799.1

SPIN
FISHING

SPIN
FISHING

by Vlad Evanoff

New York: A. S. Barnes and Company, Inc.
London: Thomas Yoseloff Ltd.

Library of Congress Catalog Card Number : 63–9371

A. S. Barnes and Company, Inc.

8 East 36th Street

New York 16, New York

Thomas Yoseloff Ltd.

18 Charing Cross Road

London W.C.2, England

9766

Printed in the United States of America

Foreword

SINCE 1946, when spinning was first introduced into the United States on a large scale, there has been a tremendous growth in the popularity of this method of fishing. With this growth there has been a great improvement in the design of spinning rods, reels, lures and lines. This book covers these improvements and also the entire field of fresh- and salt-water spinning tackle. Here you'll find the latest dope on the rods, reels, lines and lures used in fresh- and salt-water spinning.

However, the mere possession of spinning tackle doesn't automatically make you a better fisherman. You must know how to use this tackle in the streams, rivers, lakes, surf and ocean. Different fresh- and salt-water fish require different baits or lures, different methods and techniques and different approaches. In the long run these will help make you a better angler than the fishing tackle itself.

But spinning tackle does help to shorten the period of apprenticeship which every angler must serve before he becomes skilled in the use of any fishing tackle. With spinning tackle you can learn to cast in a short time, you fool the fish more easily and you can cast much smaller and lighter lures.

So I urge those who have never tried spinning to go out and buy a rod, reel, line and lures, and to use them the first chance they get. This book will tell you which tackle is best for your purposes. The angler who already has used spinning tackle can learn more about the improvements and refinements made in this field in recent years. This book, if read with care and consulted often, will provide most of the information needed to become a better spin fisherman.

VLAD EVANOFF

5

Acknowledgements

THE AUTHOR wishes to thank the following companies which supplied information and photos which helped in the writing of this book : The Garcia Corporation, Art Wire and Stamping Company, South Bend Tackle Company, Langley Corporation, Sunset Fishing Lines, Shakespeare Company, The Enterprise Manufacturing Company, True Temper Corporation, Wright and McGill, Charles F. Orvis Company, Sargent and Company, Stan Gibbs Lures, James Heddon's Sons, American Pad and Textile Company, Waterloo Valve and Spring Company.

Also the following, for sending photos : The Bahamas News Bureau, State of New York Conservation Dept., Florida State News Bureau, Oregon State Highway Dept.

CONTENTS

7

SPIN
FISHING

1

Why Spinning?

By now most anglers know that spinning or spin fishing has become the most popular method of fresh-water fishing in this country. Spin fishing has also become more and more popular in salt water, and today in many parts of the country along the coasts more salt-water anglers are using spin tackle than any other type. Surf anglers, especially, on both the East and West Coasts have really accepted spinning in a big way.

This growth in the popularity of spin-tackle fishing is amazing when you realize that it has all happened since World War II. It took a century or more for bait-casting tackle to reach the same popularity in this country. Yet spinning tackle accomplished the same thing in less than a dozen years.

Why is spinning so popular? Well, to understand it we should know a bit about the background of spinning. Ever since the earliest times, centuries ago, when man first began fishing for fun and sport he has been searching for a fishing method which could cast his lure or bait out to the fish in the most efficient manner.

First the fishermen tried ordinary hand lines or "drop" lines. But casting was a chore and the lines were good mostly for live-bait fishing. Then they started using long poles and short lines.

11

You could toss a lure out several feet and work it for a short distance. But you were always close to the fish.

Anglers also experimented with revolving-spool reels or "winches," which were the forerunners of the modern bait-casting reel. Larger models were made for salt-water fishing. But even up to the present day such reels require more or less skill in order to cast without trouble.

Fly fishing with heavy fly lines was also developed and skilled anglers could cast fair distances. But, even with the best modern equipment, fly casting is heavy work for the wrist and arm and is used only for very light lures.

In the meantime, all during the seventeenth, eighteenth and nineteenth centuries other anglers tinkered around with the "fixed-spool" principle, where the line is wound around a cylinder and then is cast so that it spills off the end of the spool. There were many variations of this principle tried in different European countries.

Finally, in 1905, an Englishman named Alfred Holden Illingworth made the first truly workable spinning reel based on this fixed-spool principle. The reel became popular and spread to France, Switzerland and other parts of Europe. It was considered so deadly it was banned from many English rivers. However, progress couldn't be stopped and better and better spinning reels were made.

Then spinning was first introduced to America by Bache Brown, who started to import the first spin reels in 1935. He gave demonstrations at sports shows, and started to market the reels and rods and wrote a booklet on fishing with spinning gear. But World War II soon came along to put a stop to all this.

It wasn't until after the War in 1946 that renewed interest in spinning began to take shape and spinning reels were imported from Europe. Such men as Joseph Bates, Jr., George Thommen, George N. Vitt, Al McLane and a few others helped to popularize this method of fishing through their books and magazine articles. Anglers became curious, then began to try spinning. They liked it, and the rush was on! Soon foreign and American manufacturers started flooding the market with imported and domestic spinning reels and rods.

Many anglers who used the older methods such as bait-casting and fly-casting tackle refused to get excited about spinning. Then, when they saw how effective it was, they jumped on the bandwagon and invested in spinning outfits. But some die-hards cursed the new method, called the reels "coffee grinders" or "contraptions" and didn't want to have anything to do with it. Attempts were even made to ban spinning outfits on trout streams.

It took a few more years to convince the opposition that spinning was here to stay and that there was not much they could do about it. Today spinning has been accepted as another method of angling by most fresh-water and salt-water fishermen. There are many reasons for the rapid growth in the popularity of spinning. It has proven to be the most versatile method yet invented. One can cast a whole range of lures, from the very lightest to those as heavy as bait-casting, in fresh water. In salt water spin-tackle fishermen can cast lures lighter than those handled by a conventional rod and yet can heave a heavy lure when needed, by merely changing rods or lines.

For live-bait fishing spinning tackle is unequaled for either fresh- or salt-water fishing. Many of these baits can be cast surprising distances without a sinker.

But what really delighted most anglers was the defeat of the old bugaboo "backlash." No longer do you need an "educated" thumb to control your casts. With a spinning reel you can forget about thumbing. The line stops flying off the reel spool as soon as the lure or bait hits the water. The result is that the average angler can cast farther with little or no trouble.

Best of all, one can learn to cast with a spinning outfit on the very first fishing trip or through some practice on dry land. It takes years to become an expert fly caster, bait caster or surf caster with conventional tackle. With a spin rod and reel everybody can master casting in a short time. Spinning is just plain easy.

This, of course, makes the spin-casting outfit ideal for the casual or weekend fisherman. Not many people get a chance to fish very often, so they don't get much practice casting with fly rods or bait-casting rods. And one needs plenty of practice to become skilled with these outfits. With a spinning outfit it makes little difference. After a "lay off" of weeks or even months, one finds his first cast is as smooth and efficient as the last one he made a long time ago.

Because spin casting is so easy it has really caught on with women, children and older folks. Before spinning, many husbands and boy friends used to have headaches trying to teach the wife or girl friend how to fly cast or bait cast. Today the average woman can pick up a spin outfit and learn to cast in a very short time. And, what's more important, go out and catch fish with it.

The kids, too, of all ages from the very youngest, soon learn how to handle a spin outfit and get their share of fun and fish.

The older folks, both men and women, also find that spin casting is just the thing for them. Many people all over the country who never fished before are taking up spinning and are getting good results. In fact, spinning tackle is made to order for them. It's light, easy to use and doesn't call for brute strength in casting or playing a fish.

Because the use of spin tackle is less tiring than other outfits, many women, children and older people find they are enjoying fishing for the first time. Casting with the fly rod or bait-casting rod can be tough on the wrist, while surf casting with conventional tackle is hard on the arms and back. But with the lighter spin rods and reels these people find that it's more pleasure than work.

Even the rugged he-man will find that the spin outfit permits

His father's boots are far too big, but no matter. He tamed that beautiful cohoe salmon on light spin tackle in the Skeena's strong current.

Experts have discovered that they can often take big fish on tiny spinning lures and hairlines, like this bass taken on an ultralight spinning outfit.

The gals have taken to spinning in a big way. Instead of spending years learning how to cast, they can now go out and start casting after a short period of instruction.

Rich guy, poor guy, celebrity or average Joe, they all get a thrill using spinning tackle. Here Dr. Milton Eisenhower, brother of the former president, catches a bonefish in the Florida Keys.

one to fish longer and make more casts during a day in the great outdoors.

Another important advantage with spin tackle is that one can use much lighter and smaller lures than with the older casting outfits. Because of the light lines and rods used, you can cast lures that are small and light in both fresh and salt water. This is very important when fishing in clear, shallow water, where big, heavy lures often frighten the fish more than they attract them. And the smaller lures often imitate the actual size of the fly, bug, insect, minnow or other fish food better than the larger lures formerly used with bait-casting tackle.

Add to this that you also use thinner, almost invisible lines, and you have a combination which many fish can't resist. Fly fishermen also use light leaders. But the heavy fly line is still highly visible and often lands with a splash or drags in the water, and this usually "puts down" the fish. The heavy salt-water lines used with conventional tackle are clearly seen in clean waters. But when you use spinning tackle the thin and less visible lines provide a definite advantage which means more and bigger fish.

Because of these lighter lines one can usually make longer casts with spin tackle than with other outfits. Of course, long casts are not always required to catch fish, but it's comforting to know you can make such casts if the need arises. And on many occasions fish are feeding far out or the best spot is on the other side of a stream. Or you may have to reach a sand bar or hole in the surf a good distance from the beach.

You not only can make longer casts but cover more water. A spin angler can stand in one spot and cover the water in a wide arc to his left or right. He doesn't have to wade into deep or dangerous water to reach such spots. Nor does he have to disturb the water by wading into casting position, as is often the case with the more conventional fly-rod fisherman.

Finally, there's the extra dividend of hooking and fighting a fish on a light line and rod which provides the maximum in thrills, fun and sport. Every strike, every run, leap, lunge and movement is telegraphed down the sensitive rod. The rod tip bends and quivers, which delights the angler and overcomes the fish at the same time.

Sure, it generally takes longer to land a fish on a spin rod than on a bait-casting or conventional surf rod. But by the same token many big fish that would have broken the line or worked loose from the hook on these older outfits are saved and landed on the spin outfit. Besides, the main objective in fishing is to have as much fun as possible. So the longer you fight a fish the more you prolong your enjoyment.

But don't get the impression that spinning tackle is perfect and a "cure-all" for all your fishing problems. Although the spin outfit has many advantages over the other types of tackle it still can't do everything. And for many fishing conditions the other outfits are superior.

One may not get backlashes using a spin reel, but other troubles sometimes occur, such as loose coils of line which spill off the reel spool and foul up the works. Or the line wraps around some reel part or the guide on the rod. One may lose more lures with spin outfits when they break off on a cast or when the lure fouls on the bottom. It must be remembered that spinning tackle is light tackle. It just won't stand the same rough handling and abuse that many other types of tackle can.

However, all these drawbacks are minor, and the spin outfit will make a person a better angler in a shorter period of time than any other type of casting tackle being used today.

The tackle alone won't do it, of course. Buying a spin outfit won't make a person a skilled angler overnight. If it did so, there would be no need for this book. You could buy a spin rod, reel, line and lures and go out and catch all the fish wanted. But that is far from being the case. There are many things to learn before one can call himself a good angler. The fishing fan will have to learn where to fish, how to locate the fish, which lures or baits to use, how to present and work them effectively, how to hook and fight the fish and how to land them. All this takes time, and we hope this book will help make that period shorter.

You can't start youngsters too young on spin fishing, according to Claude Roberts, general sales manager for Langley Corporation, shown giving Roberta Ann Brazell of San Diego a few pointers in handling a spin-casting reel.

Langley Photo

2

Fresh-water Spinning Reels

As EXPLAINED in the previous chapter on the background of spinning, the development of the spin reel gave us the relatively new method of spin-tackle fishing. The rest of the tackle used in spinning, such as the rod, line, lures and accessories, aren't too different from similar items used in other fresh- and salt-water methods. But the spinning reel is radically different from the other reels. It is really the most important single tackle item used in spin fishing. So more attention should be focused on the spinning reel than the other tackle.

The basic difference between a spinning reel and a conventional revolving-spool reel is that the spin reel has a stationary or "fixed spool" which doesn't revolve when casting. In the conventional bait-casting or surf-casting reel you have a revolving spool which turns as the line flies off the reel during the cast. This spool must be controlled with the thumb or some sort of gadget which keeps it revolving at the proper speed. If it goes too fast the line doesn't keep pace in leaving the spool and a bad tangle or backlash results. If the spool slows down too much you don't get any distance. And a revolving spool needs a fairly heavy lure or weight to overcome he inertia of the spool and line and start

20

it moving. So getting any distance with light lures on a revolving spool is difficult.

The spinning reel, on the other hand, has no revolving spool. The line leaves the stationary spool freely off the end and just coils off without any movement of the reel parts. You don't have to use your thumb or fingers to control the cast. The line flies off as long as the lure or weight exerts a pull. The minute it hits the water the line stops moving off the reel spool. It's so simple that you can cast on the darkest night or blindfolded, and make long, perfect casts every time.

Since there is no revolving spool to be started moving by the lure or weight, the line on a spinning reel requires very little pull to get it going. A tiny, light lure or weight will start the line moving off the reel and will carry it to a surprising distance. This means that the spin-fishing angler is free from those pesky backlashes and that he can cast very light lures. These are two big advantages he has over the anglers using revolving bait-casting or surf-casting reels.

Another big difference between spin reels and most revolving-spool reels is that the spin reel hangs below the rod with the line guides also downward, while conventional reels are attached above the rod. And spin reels usually come with the crank handle on the left side, while revolving-spool reels mostly have right-handed cranks.

It seems awkward and strange at first to reel with your left hand, especially if you are right handed and have been using the right hand for reeling all these years. But this soon disappears, and in a short time it seems like you have been reeling with your left hand all your life.

The big advantage of left-hand reeling is that you can cast a spin rod with your right hand, then immediately grasp the reel handle and wind with your left hand. The rod doesn't change hands and you are ready for action. With a bait-casting or surf-casting rod and revolving-spool reels you cast with your right hand or on the right side, then transfer the rod and reel to your left hand or left side before you can turn the handle efficiently. You also have to transfer the rod and reel with the "spin-casting" or "push-button" type reels, but for the moment we are mainly discussing the true open-faced or closed-faced reels which hang below the rod.

For those anglers who are in the habit of reeling with the right hand and refuse to change, there are plenty of spinning reels on the market with handles for right-handed cranking. Some reels are interchangeable and you can attach the handle on either side.

As an aid to buying a spinning reel the angler should become acquainted with its important parts and features. There are basically three types of spinning reels which work on the fixed-spool principle. The first is the "open-faced" or "open-spool" spinning reel. The second is the "closed-faced" spinning reel, which mounts under the rod. The third is the "spin-casting" or "push-button" reel, which mounts above the rod like a bait-casting reel. This chapter will cover the first two reels, which mount under the rod. The spin-casting rods and reels will be covered in Chapter 6.

The open-spool reel, as the name implies, has the spool exposed so that you can see the line. This reel had a head start, since it was developed first, and at present they still outnumber the closed spool type reels both in numbers and models for both fresh- and salt-water fishing.

An important part of any spinning reel is the line pick-up, which catches the line and then winds it back on the reel spool after a cast. The earlier spinning reels had a "manual" pick-up, and spin reels with such pick-ups are still used to a certain extent. Here the angler uses the right index finger to catch the line after a cast, then winds it back on the reel. This method is the most nearly foolproof, and a few anglers prefer it to other methods. After practice the movements become automatic and

*South Bend No. 22 closed-faced spinning reel has diamond-cut
drive gear. Holds 110yds. of 6-lb. test line*

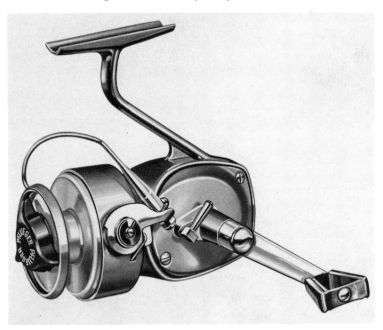

*Pflueger Freeflite open-faced spinning reel is of medium size but
holds a lot of line—200yds. of 8-lb. test.*

Quick Microlite fresh-water spinning reel is imported from Germany by Bradlow, Inc. of Los Angeles, California. It can be changed for either right- or left-hand cranking, and holds 175 yds. of 6-lb. test line.

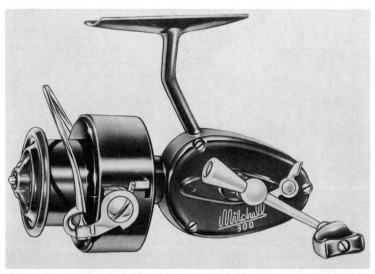

The Garcia Mitchell 300 is an old favorite for most fresh-water and light salt-water fishing. It is a typical open-faced reel.

the line is picked up with little trouble. Spin reels with manual pick-ups are a bit cheaper in price than reels with automatic pick-ups. Another big advantage of the manual pick-up is that it results in a sturdier reel with fewer parts to get out of order. And there are fewer places for the line to tangle.

Another type of pick-up is the finger or arm type, which was found on many earlier models. It is still popular with some salt-water anglers, who use large spinning reels with such pick-ups. Here a short, curved arm swings into position and catches the line for winding back on the spool. This is automatic and just requires the turning of the handle of the reel to pick up the line. The big disadvantage of the arm pick-up are that it often misses the line and sometimes the line tangles around the arm. And the pick-up fingers or arms are often bent out of shape.

Today the most popular type of pick-up is the third type, called the "full bail." Here you have a wire hoop which catches the line and throws it into the groove or roller when the reel handle is turned. This is automatic, too, and a spin reel with a good working bail pick-up is very convenient to use. Expert anglers like it because it is fast working and is especially handy when fishing with lures which must be reeled back the instant they hit the water. Beginners like the bail pick-up because it is easy to use and requires little practice.

Many spin reels with bail pick-ups can be converted to manual in a short time. This is done by removing the bail and adding a conversion unit, which is sold at a modest price. With such a reel you can try both manual and bail pick-ups, and see which you prefer. And if anything goes wrong with the bail you can still fish with the reel by changing to the manual.

Many reels have a roller over which the line runs when retrieved. This roller takes a lot of wear, especially when retrieving heavy lures or fighting big fish in salt water. On good reels these rollers turn freely. The roller should, of course, be made of very hard metal, sapphire or agate. Otherwise a grove will soon appear where the line rubs against it.

Another feature which makes the spinning reel different from most of the other fresh-water reels is the friction clutch or drag. This is a mechanical device which enables the fish to take the line out under a steady tension and permits the angler to handle the fish more easily and tire it out sooner. Drags vary somewhat in construction, but the majority make use of some sort of slipping clutch which exerts pressure on the spool. These drags can be adjusted so that the amount of pressure on the spool can be regulated. On most reels this consists of a wing nut in front of the spool which can be tightened or loosened. But other reels have various attachments at different parts of the reel for controlling the drag.

Of course, drags have been used on conventional salt-water reels for a long time. And some bait-casting reels had drags for fresh-water use before spinning reels appeared here. In the early days these drags were considered unsporting and the majority of fresh-water fishermen used bait-casting reels without drags. In salt-water big-game fishing and surf fishing, reels with drags have been popular for many years.

Because of the light lines used in spinning, the drag is a vital part of the spinning reel. When a fish wants to run, a good drag enables him to do so without placing too much strain on the line. So an important consideration when choosing a spin reel is that the drag should be smooth. And it should keep the tension at which it has been set. If you are fishing with the heavier spin lines for fish which don't run or leap much, then a smooth drag is not so important. But for light lines and especially "ultra-light" spinning and for active game fish, the drag should be smooth with no jerking or binding. The drag should have a gradual adjustment instead of a sudden one. In other words when you increase the drag or decrease it you should be able to do it a little at a time. On some reels even a slight twist of the knob will increase

Garcia ABU 505 closed-faced spinning reel has a star drag and oscillating spool. It holds 125yds. of 8-lb. Super-Platyl line.

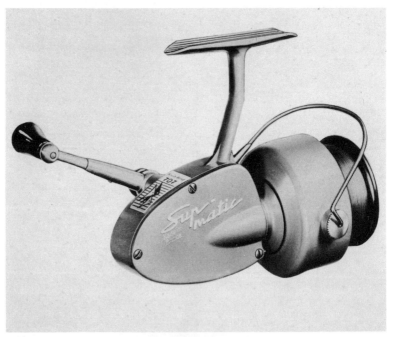

South Bend French-made "Sup-matic 707" features a push-button 2-speed retrieve. It has a spool capacity of 300yds. of 8-lb. test line.

the drag too much. If this happens during a fight with a fish you may break the line.

The setting you use and how you set the drag is a controversial subject among spin anglers. Some like to fish with a light drag; others prefer as much drag as the line will take. However, the best way to test the drag and set it is to rig up your spin rod and reel as for actual fishing. Then get someone to run off about 50 or 75 feet of line. If you are alone you can tie the end of the line to a tree or other solid support, and then back up and let out the line. Now tighten your drag slightly and back up. Keep backing up and tightening your drag until the rod takes its maximum bend. When it does bend almost as far as it will go, try backing up again. The line should still slip off the spool, but not too easily. Now you have about the maximum fishing drag that particular line will stand with a safety margin.

If you are fishing for small species which do not run, you can leave that setting. For example, when fishing for pan fish such as sunfish with sinkers and live bait, a tight drag is all right. However, if you are fishing for fish which run a long way, leap and otherwise put up an active scrap, you can loosen the drag more.

Many experienced anglers claim that once the drag is set it should be left that way. This may be true most of the time, but there are conditions when loosening or tightening a drag will be necessary. For example, when fishing with a fairly loose drag and a fish suddenly starts to head downstream for the rapids below and you can't follow him. Or when a fish tries to reach some weeds or a log and you want to keep him away, it may be a wise move to tighten the drag and try to turn him or at least slow him down. And if an active fish starts taking much line you should loosen up after he has run off about half the line on your spool. A drag setting for a full spool of line may be too much for a half-empty spool.

On the other hand, when you have a fish licked and he turns

over on his side near the boat or shore you may have to tighten the drag in order to bring him close enough for netting or beaching. This is especially true in rivers or streams where the current is running strong.

It isn't always necessary to tighten the drag by turning the knob or lever. You can exert pressure on the spool with your forefinger against the lip or flange. In fact, this is usually the best way to add pressure during a fight with a fish. And it is about the only way you can apply pressure when using ultralight tackle and the thin hairlines.

Another useful device found on most spinning reels is the antireverse lock. When this is in the "On" position it prevents the reel handle from turning backward. Some anglers like it so much that they leave it in the "On" position all the time. But this isn't necessary when casting with artificial lures. It is mainly needed for fighting a fish, and should be put on as soon as a fish is hooked. Some reels have an automatic antireverse, which takes over. An antireverse is also useful when you are fishing alone and want to land or beach a fish. Then you can take your hand off the reel handle and use it for gaffing or netting a fish. The antireverse is also used when trolling or still fishing. Here you often put the rod down and with the antireverse in the "On" position any strike is against the drag. Most spin reels with the antireverse on also have an audible click which warns of a bite or strike.

When the fishing outfit is not being used it should also have the antireverse on, otherwise the handle will turn and line will be taken off the reel when it gets caught on anything.

As for spool sizes or capacities, you rarely have to worry about this in fresh-water fishing. Most of the regular open-faced spinning reels hold more than enough line on their spools. Some reels have spools of two sizes, one holding more than the other. For light lines and small fish you can use the smaller spools. While for heavier lines and big fish you can use the larger one.

More important than the line capacity is an extra spool or

two. These can be filled with lines of different sizes. One reel spool can hold 4-lb. test, the other 6-lb. test and a third spool can have a still heavier test. For this reason it pays to buy a reel which has a quick system for changing spools without too much trouble.

The size and weight of the reel itself may vary. Spinning reels usually run from 4 to 12 oz. in weight for fresh-water fishing. The light ones are ideal with the lightest spin rods, light lines and for small- or medium-sized fish. The lightest reels are usually made from nylon, plastic or similar materials. Or the reels are made very small for ultralight fishing, which also cuts down on the weight. If you want to try ultralight fishing you can now find several small reels from which to choose. Two of the first reels to appear on the market were the Alcedo Micron, distributed by the Continental Arms Company, and the Mignon 33, imported by the Rockland Tackle Company. Another popular reel for this fishing is the Langley Spinlite, made by the Langley Corporation. The Garcia Corporation makes the Mitchell 308 for what they call "Ultra Sports" fishing. These small reels usually range from about 5 to 8 oz. in weight and are made to match the featherweight rods and hairlines with which they are used.

Ultralight reels and tackle are best for the more advanced or experienced angler. For the beginner, the somewhat larged-sized reels are better, especially if you want only one spinning reel for "all-around" fishing. With these you can use heavier rods, lines and lures as needed.

For heavy-duty fresh-water spinning you may need a larger fresh-water spinning reel or a salt-water model. Only for certain types of fishing, such as big catfish, sturgeon and carp, do you require such big reels and lines testing up to 20lbs. or more. Anglers seeking pike and muskies also use the larger spinning reels.

The closed-spool or "American" type reel was developed in this country. When the first open-faced reels appeared some

manufacturers felt that they could be improved or at least simpli-
fied. The result was the closed-faced spinning reel, which hangs
below the rod. This was followed by the spin-casting reel which
is mounted above the rod.

The open-spool reel, of course, has the spool exposed; and the
line spirals off in coils. In the closed-spool type the spool is
covered entirely or partially by a cover, usually cone- or cupped-
shaped, which hides the spool. The line comes out of a hole on
front of the cone. The open-faced reels require larger guides cn
the spinning rod, whereas the closed-faced reel casts well with
smaller guides.

Another big difference between the two is that the closed-faced
reels do not use exposed line pick-ups such as bails or arms.
Instead, they generally have some kind of internal pick-up pin
which moves out of the way when the cast is being made. Then,
when the reel handle is turned, the pin emerges and catches the
line, to wind it back on the spool. The principle of casting is the
same as with the open-spool reel since the spool doesn't revolve
on the cast. So you can cast just as easily with the closed-type
reels as with the open type, with no backlashes.

The closed-type reels also have drags which can be adjusted
for playing a fish. Most of them have smooth drags which do a
good job on most fresh-water fish.

The closed-faced reels we are interested in here are those which
hang below the rod like the open-faced reels. They usually come
with the handle or crank on the left-hand side. You cast with
your right hand and reel in with your left. However, you can
also obtain such reels with handles on the right side for right-
hand cranking.

Which reels are better? Which should you choose for your
fresh-water fishing? Well, it all depends on the angler and the
type of fishing he plans to do. When closed-faced reels first came
out they had some defects, such as the line binding on the narrow
spool or twisting badly on the retrieve or being pinched or ruined

by some part of the reel. These reels have been improved greatly in recent years, however, and are now practical, efficient fishing tools.

The main disadvantage of a closed-spool reel is that it doesn't cast very light lures quite as far as does an open-faced reel. And you can't use very light lines on closed-faced reels. It also takes a bit more time to change spools on a closed-spool reel. For the angler who plans to fish ultralight or wants to obtain the maximum casting distances, the open-faced spinning reel is best.

But the closed-faced reels are simple, durable and almost foolproof. They are easier and simpler to operate, with fewer manual motions to master or remember. So for the average angler or beginner who doesn't spend much time fishing or casting, these reels are ideal. They are perfect, for example, for most women and kids who go fishing a few times a year.

More important than the type of reel is the quality of the reel and whether parts are readily available for repairs. Here you can't go by price alone. The manufacturer's name is more of a help. But the best way to choose a reel is to find out from an expert angler which one he uses and prefers. Or get a reliable tackle dealer to recommend a good reel. Check and find out whether the reel can be repaired quickly if it gets out of order. There is nothing more exasperating than to find out that you can't obtain parts for your reel. Or that repairs will take weeks or even months, as has happened with some imported reels in the past.

3

Salt-water Spinning Reels

THE FIRST spinning reels used in salt water in this country were the smaller fresh-water models first imported from Europe. Then, larger special salt-water models started arriving from abroad and American manufacturers started making the bigger reels. Now the variety of salt-water reels, both imported and domestic, is so great that there's a model for almost any kind of ocean fishing.

It's true that many fresh-water reels are being used in salt water, especially with the lighter spin rods which are cast with one hand. There is nothing wrong with using such a spinning reel in salt water, provided it stands up and is used mostly for light fishing. But many fresh-water spinning reels can't take it when exposed to salt-water fishing conditions. Others corrode badly or do not hold enough line. So, in the long run, it's much safer to use a spinning reel specially designed for salt-water fishing.

Salt-water spinning reels come in various sizes and weights from about 8 oz. up to 26 oz. or more. We can divide them into three classes as an aid to choosing the best size for the fishing you plan to do. There are light, medium and heavy reels. The light salt-water spinning reels range from about 8 to 12 oz. and are best for light fishing and light lures and small- or medium-sized fish.

Not too many reels in this class are made specially for salt water, so you'll usually find spinning reels which are popular in fresh water being used for this light fishing. Such reels hold anywhere from 150 to 300 yds. of 6, 8 or 10-lb. test line. The light spinning reel is ideal for use from boats and shore for one-hand casting of light lures for small- and medium-sized fish.

The medium salt-water spinning reels will range from about 12 to 20 oz. in weight. They have larger spools, stronger parts and gears, and are made to cast heavier lures and fight bigger fish. The reels in this class will hold anywhere from 150 to 400 yds. of line. Lines testing 12 to 25 lbs. are usually used with these reels. The reels in the medium-weight class can be used for fishing from boats, piers, bridges, shore or surf for a wide variety of fish. They are used with two-handed spinning rods from boats or surf and you can cast good distances with such outfits.

Heavy salt-water spinning reels will range from 20 to 26 oz. or more and have extra large spools, heavy-duty parts and gears, and include the largest spinning reels made today. Such big jobs will hold anywhere from 250 to 800 yds. of line testing from 15 to 40 lbs. Such reels are designed for the heaviest surf fishing and long casts and are also used offshore for the smaller- and medium-sized game fish such as albacore, amberjack, sailfish, white marlin, striped marlin and sharks.

Salt-water spinning reels are similar in construction to the fresh-water reels discussed in the previous section. They have the same features, such as drags, line pick-ups, anti-reverse, inter-changeable spools, etc. But these are usually larger and much stronger than those found on fresh-water reels. They have to be able to take the sudden or prolonged strains of working heavy lures and fighting big fish. The wear and tear on such reels is often terrific and poor materials or construction show up quickly under actual fishing conditions.

The other important differences between fresh-water spin reels and salt-water models is that the salt-water reels are made from materials which resist the corrosion of salt water. Various metals and plastics are used for this purpose. Some of the reels are better than others in this respect, but most of them require constant care to prevent corrosion.

In choosing a salt-water spinning reel the friction clutch or drag is a vital consideration. With fresh-water reels you can often get away with using drags which jerk or bind, especially for the smaller species. But in salt-water fishing you never know when you might hook one of the bigger, faster-moving species. Some of these, such as the bonefish, tarpon, amberjack, barracuda, yellowtail, albacore, striped bass and channel bass, will rip off many yards of line at a fast pace. Not to mention the heavier fish, such as marlin and sailfish, which can take hundreds of feet of line at a terrific speed. When going after such fish a smooth, constant drag is a must. Otherwise you will lose fish after fish.

You can set your drag as described in the fresh-water spinning reel section. However, you will find it necessary to change your drag setting on many occasions while fishing in salt water. The fish run bigger, have tougher jaws and in addition you often have to contend with heavy surf, strong currents and tides. For example, when fishing with small, light lures and tiny hooks you can often use a light drag to hook a fish. The same goes for fish with soft mouths. Yet when you change lures and use larger, heavier ones with big hooks you need a tighter drag to drive home the hook. This is especially true of fish with tough jaws and mouths.

When fishing for fish which start off on long, fast runs when hooked, you need a fairly light drag. If a fish takes out a lot of line you may even have to loosen the drag still more. In fact, in fishing for such a fast-running fish which takes long runs you often need two men in a boat. While one man is fighting the fish the other handles the boat and follows the fish when there is danger that the reel may be emptied.

On the other hand, when you have a fish near the boat or

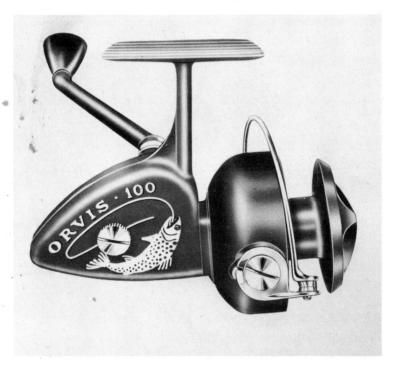

*The Orvis 100 spinning reel is made in Italy and is widely used
for light salt-water spinning. It holds 250yds. of 6-lb. test line.*

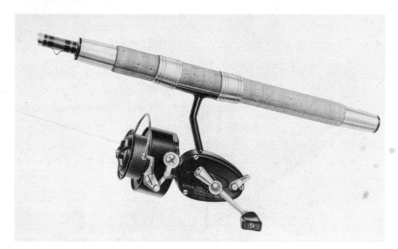

Garcia Mitchell 330 features an automatic full-bail pick-up. The bail, instead of your finger, holds the line at casting and releases the line automatically.

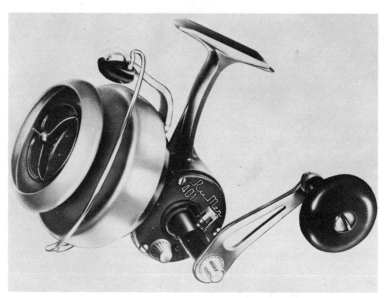

The Ru Mer 401 is a large salt-water spinning reel suitable for surf and boat fishing. It holds 220yds. of 24-lb. test line. It can be quickly transformed from a full bail to manual operation.

shore ready for boating or landing, you often have to tighten the drag in order to bring him in. This is especially true when beaching a fish in the surf or when fishing in a strong tide or current. Of course, you should never tighten the drag so much that no line comes off.

There are times, however, when bottom fishing from a boat, pier or bridge for small species which have to be brought in quickly or lifted some distance, when a very tight drag can be used. This can be done if you are using fairly strong, heavy lines. But when fishing for the larger game fish the drag setting should always be well below the strength of the line. A sudden leap or run can always be expected until the fish is completely licked or boated.

Salt-water spinning reels with full-bail pick-ups are the most popular. But some anglers prefer reels with finger or arm pick-ups or manual operation. A reel with a properly working full bail is a pleasure to use and is preferred by surf anglers and others who cast lures or metal squids and jigs which must be reeled back almost the instant they hit the water. With a manually operated pick-up there's a split second or so before the line is caught and the retrieve is started. This often means that the lure sinks a few feet, and in rocky areas this means a fouled lure, which is often lost.

But reels with full-bail or finger pick-ups sometimes cause trouble when they are bent out of shape or when springs break or weaken and lines tangle around the finger or arm. A manual pick-up, on the other hand, almost always works and won't let the angler down during a crucial moment. One disadvantage of some manual-type reels is that the line has a tendency to fall out of the roller when there is any slack present. Yet some salt-water anglers swear by the manual models and use them skillfully.

The roller on salt-water reels should revolve freely, if it's supposed to do so, and should be made from a hard substance such as sapphire, genuine agate, hard chrome or other tough metal which resists wear and grooving. Rollers made of soft metal or those which don't turn freely quickly wear when fishing for big fish and using heavy lures.

Salt-water reels also have an antireverse lock, and this is even more important in salt-water fishing than in fresh-water. Most anglers fishing with bait and sinker on the bottom leave the anti-reverse in the "On" position at all times, so that they can remove their hand from the reel handle. If you use your salt-water spinning reel for trolling you should also leave the anti-reverse on most of the time. The same thing should be done if you are jigging with jigs or other lures. Some surf anglers also like to leave the antireverse in the "On" position most of the time while casting and reeling in the lures. Others like to leave in the "Off" position while casting and retrieving, but put it on immediately after a fish is hooked. And the antireverse should be left in the "On" position when the rod and reel is being carried or transported from one spot to another.

Spools and spool capacity are also important in salt-water spin fishing. The spools must be strong, to take the strain of fighting a big fish. Nylon lines, especially monofilament, when packed tight on a reel during a fight with a fish, exert a lot of pressure and can break a weak spool. The spool should hold enough line for the fishing you plan to do. For small species and light fishing they don't have to be too big. But for surf fishing, offshore fishing and long casts you need the largest capacity spools. Most fishing done in salt water calls for the use of lines testing from 8 to 30 lbs. In the heavier tests you can't get much line on a small spool. And you don't get much casting distance if your line falls rapidly below the flanges of the spool.

For offshore fishing you also need the larger spinning reels with big spools which hold plenty of line. More and more heavy-duty salt-water spinning reels are being made today, and with the new, thin-diameter lines the problem of enough line on the spool is being solved for most situations in salt-water fishing.

Langley "Spinator" salt-water spinning reel has been restyled and has a self-centering bail, two-point shaft suspension for solid bearing support. It holds 300yds. of 20-lb. test line.

The Penn spinning reel for salt-water fishing is the first spinning reel made by a company long-famous for its conventional reels. It is corrosion resistant, has stainless-steel gears, automatic bail lock. Holds 250yds. of 20-lb. test line.

One safe guide in buying a salt-water spinning reel is to stay with the reputable manufacturer who has been in business for a long time and has a good reputation. Make sure that spare parts are available and repair service is reasonably fast.

The care given salt-water spinning reels will determine how long they last and how they operate. The reel can be washed in running fresh water after using in salt water. This will remove most of the salt deposits. Then the reel should be wiped dry and oiled at all friction points, such as the handle knob, the roller, each end of the bait pick-up, etc. This is best done before and after each fishing trip.

About once or twice each season the reel can be taken apart and the gear housing can be cleaned with gasoline or kerosene. (Do this outdoors, if possible.) Then the reel should be repacked with reel grease made especially for fishing reels.

It doesn't pay to fool around with the gears and drag washers, springs, etc., unless you are certain you know what you are doing. If anything goes wrong take the reel to a fishing-tackle store specializing in such repairs or send it back to the factory.

In salt-water fishing even the best reels sometimes fail on a fishing trip, and unless repairs can be made quickly in the field you are out of luck. Some reel companies sell small repair kits of spare parts to replace those that give the most trouble. While it's a good idea to carry such kits, an even better suggestion is to carry in your car a spare reel or two filled with line. When there's a run of fish on you haven't got much time to make repairs, and can save time by simply switching reels.

4

Fresh-water Spinning Rods

WHEN IT COMES TO buying a good spinning rod, the angler has less chance of going wrong today than in the earlier days when spinning was first introduced in this country. Now many American rod manufacturers are turning out fine spin rods for all kinds of fishing. If you buy such a rod from one of the reputable companies you'll find you're getting your money's worth. With proper care such a rod will last for many years.

Fresh-water spin rods are made mostly from hollow glass, solid glass and a few from split bamboo. The hollow-glass rods are easily the most popular. They combine ruggedness with light weight and good action. If you are buying your first spinning rod you can't go wrong by getting a hollow- or tubular-glass rod. The same thing is true if you can afford only one rod.

Spinning rods are also made of solid glass. These are usually cheaper in price and very strong. They are often satisfactory in the shorter lengths up to six feet or so. Beyond that length, or if they are improperly designed, they tend to be top-heavy and slow in action. Solid-glass rods are also somewhat heavier in general than hollow-glass rods of the same taper and length. If you want a cheap, second rod to use for trolling or fishing with sinkers, a solid-glass rod will often serve the purpose. Many people also buy them for youngsters who are apt to ruin a good, expensive rod.

When spinning was first introduced, split-bamboo rods were very common. Now they have almost disappeared from the market, although a few are still being made. The cheaper bamboo rods just couldn't compete with glass rods on the market. However, in the more expensive rods, a good split-bamboo rod is still considered a fine fishing tool. Many expert anglers claim that they have a better action than glass rods. But the difference is so slight that it doesn't mean much.

Bamboo rods will break more easily than glass, and require more care, such as drying and varnishing. They also take a set (permanent bend) after being used a long time or strained. But impregnated bamboo rods, such as those made by the Charles F. Orvis Company, are waterproofed with Bakelite Resin and are not affected by water, humidity or heat. If you do buy a bamboo spinning rod, buy a good one. When it comes to bamboo rods, only the best are worth having.

All spin rods look very much alike and only if you know what to look for can you separate the poor ones from the good ones. Of course, when it comes to the glass blank itself you have to depend on the reputation of the rod manufacturer or whoever makes the raw blanks. The finished rod will depend on the type of glass used, the kind of bonding agent, taper, diameter and thickness of the glass blank. The cheaper rods are made from a cloth of coarser glass fibers or filaments, and fewer layers are used. The result is that the cheaper rod has less glass and more resin. The better rods, on the other hand, have finer glass fibers and more layers are used, with less resin or other bonding agent.

The better rods also have more expensive component parts or fittings, such as ferrules, guides, reel seats and handles. Ferrules on the better rods are usually made from nickel silver, stainless steel or anodized aluminium or similar alloys. The cheaper rods usually have plated-brass ferrules.

The type of reel seat or fastening used to hold the reel also varies with the manufacturer. Today the trend is toward the fixed-locking reel seats similar to those that are used on salt-water rods. These have a screw thread and knurled ring which holds a spinning reel securely in place. Such fixed reel seats are made of light metals, such as anodized aluminium on the light rods and of heavier stainless steel or plated brass on the heavier rods.

In the beginning most fresh-water spinning rods had two metal rings sliding on the cork handle, to hold the reel in place. The rings are forced over the feet of the spinning reel to hold it firmly against the cork. This works fine if the cork is new and there is a tight fit. But it tends to compress the cork handle and leaves indentations. After a while the sliding metal rings may not hold the reel securely.

The main advantage of using the metal rings is that they allow the angler to change the position of his reel on the handle. But in actual practice very few anglers take advantage of this and usually use the reel in the same position most of the time. Nowadays the sliding rings are used mostly on the lightest fresh-water spinning rods to cut down weight. But to play safe, many anglers use some kind of tape over the rings, to hold the reel more securely.

Another system of holding the reel in place consists of a pair of rings around a moveable metal or plastic shoe. There is a section cut out for the reel foot to fit into. This type of reel seat also slides up and down on the reel handle, and enables you to place the reel in various positions.

The cork grip or handle on fresh-water spinning rods also varies in quality and construction. A cheap rod has cork which is soft and spongy or pitted. Some rods also have handles or grips made of a cork composition. But the most expensive rods usually have fine quality cork which is firm, free of pits and glued so tightly together in a series of cork rings that it looks like one molded section. Good cork also feels smooth and silky in your hand.

The guides on a rod are also important. There should be enough guides to take the strain of casting and playing a fish along the whole length of the rod. This will vary according to the length and stiffness of a rod, but usually no less than five guides are needed. These should be properly spaced. This can be quickly tested by running a line through the guides, then bending the rod after the end of the line is tied to something. The line should conform evenly to the bend of the rod and should not touch the rod at any point.

Guides should be made from some hard material, such as chrome-plated tungsten steel or Carboloy. Some rods also have stainless-steel guides, and these are excellent if the steel is hard. A few spinning rods also have genuine agate guides. These are very hard and are not grooved by the line. But agate is easily broken and cracked when hit sharply against a rock or other hard object.

The guides should graduate in size from a large guide near the handle to progressively smaller ones toward the tip. This is especially important when using open-faced spinning reels. The wide circular motion of the line leaving the reel must be narrowed down. And because the spinning reel hangs well away from the rod, the guides should be mounted on supports which keep them away from the rod. This helps prevent line slap against the rod.

The most common type of guide consists of a ring supported by four legs fused to two feet which lay against the rod. Some of the larger guides also have a bridge support attached to the ring as added reinforcement. Another type of guide has a single piece of wire twisted to form a ring and two legs. Still another type has a ring which is cocked at an angle to form a funnel and has only one foot instead of the usual two. This guide allows more flexibility and also prevents the line from fouling around it.

When a group of anglers gets together and starts talking about rod "action" you'll quickly notice that they can't seem to agree what kind of action or length a rod should have. This is only natural, since each angler has his own preference. They don't fish the same waters, or seek the same fish or use the same lures, so how can they agree on rod action or length? To make matters worse, people vary in height, weight and strength. They also have different casting styles. All these things must be taken into consideration when choosing a spinning rod.

The first step is to choose a rod which has the proper design for accurate and effortless spin casting. Actual casting with such a rod, with lures of different weights, will give the experienced spin fisherman a good idea of the action.

The next step is to decide where you are going to fish most of the time, what weight and type of lures you will be using and the size of the average fish you will catch. Are you fishing mainly for sport and looking for the most fun and action? Or are you mostly interested in catching fish and not losing too many?

To simplify matters, we'll break fresh-water spinning rods down into three main groups: light, medium and heavy. The light spinning rod will range from about 6 to $7\frac{1}{2}$ ft. and will weigh about $2\frac{1}{2}$ to 4 oz. They cast lures weighing from $\frac{1}{8}$ to $\frac{3}{8}$ oz. and are used mainly with lines testing 3 or 4 lbs. This rod is the one to get if you plan to do mostly trout fishing in small streams and lakes. It is ideal for any small- or medium-sized fish in open waters, such as pan fish, pickerel, bass and most trout.

For the beginner just taking up spin fishing, the medium rod is the most suitable. It is the nearest thing to an "all-around" fresh-water spinning rod. You can cast the lightest lures for short distances and even handle a heavier lure, if needed. In other words, if you can buy only one rod get the medium fresh-water spinning rod. Such a rod will run from 6 to $7\frac{1}{2}$ ft. in length and

Rods made for open-faced spinning reels should have graduating large ring guides like these Garcia-made guides.

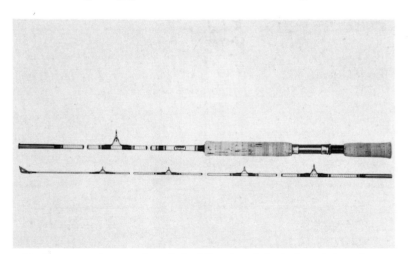

Shakespeare Companion Spin Wonderod is designed for closed-faced under-the-rod reels. It is 7ft. long and handles lures from $\frac{1}{8}$ to $\frac{1}{2}$ oz.

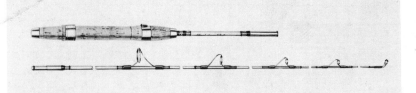

Heddon "Mark III" ultralight spinning rod is 5 ft. long and handles lures from $\frac{1}{20}$ to $\frac{1}{8}$ oz.

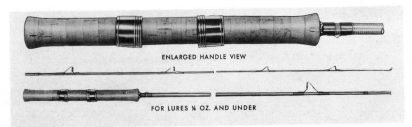

ENLARGED HANDLE VIEW

FOR LURES ⅛ OZ. AND UNDER

Wright & McGill "Feather Light" spinning rod is made for extra-light spinning and is 6½ ft. long.

ENLARGED HANDLE VIEW

Wright & McGill "Spin-Champ" hollow-glass spinning rod comes in two pieces and is 8 ft. long.

weigh from 4 to 6 oz. It performs best when casting lures from $\frac{1}{4}$ to $\frac{5}{8}$ oz. Lines testing 4 or 6 lbs. are used with the medium rod. The medium rod can be used for most of the fish found in fresh water, such as big trout, black bass, walleyes, small steelhead, small pike and big pan fish. It also makes a good bait-fishing rod with natural baits such as worms, minnows and frogs, with or without light sinkers.

Heavy fresh-water spinning rods come in lengths from $6\frac{1}{2}$ to 9 ft. They may range in weight from 5 to 10 oz. and may be used with lines testing from 8 to 20 lbs. The shorter rods may be light enough to cast with one hand, but the longer, heavier ones will require two-hand casting. Some of these rods will handle lures up to $1\frac{1}{2}$ to 2 oz. in weight. The longer rods are also used where long casts may be required with such lures. You can use them for big black bass, pike, muskellunge, lake trout, steelhead, Pacific salmon. They can also be used for bottom fishing with bait for such fish as catfish and carp.

There is another class of rods which have become very popular in recent years. These are the so-called ultralight or UL rods, which range from 4 to 6 ft. in length and weigh only an ounce or two. They are used with hairlines testing only $\frac{1}{2}$ lb. to 3 lbs., and can cast lures weighing from $\frac{1}{32}$ to $\frac{1}{4}$ oz. Such a rod must be used with the smallest and light spinning reels. The whole outfit, rod and reel combined, may weigh only 7 or 8 oz. Such a feather-weight outfit is a pleasure to use because of this lightness, and you obtain the ultimate in sport with even the smallest fish. It is a deadly way to fish when the streams are low and the waters clear. It can cast the lightest and tiniest lures to catch trout, bass and pan fish.

Naturally there are limitations to the use of an ultralight tackle which must be observed. It is not an outfit for all-round fishing or for waters where there are obstructions such as rocks, logs, weeds, sunken trees, etc. It is not the best rod to use where the fish run big and the current is very strong. The use of such light tackle also requires quite a bit of practice and skill, which may take some time to acquire. So a beginner is better off with a heavier outfit until he has gained some experience.

The length of the rod you will buy will depend on your own personal preference and the type of fishing you do. Most spinning rods are made in 6, 6½ and 7-ft. lengths with the 6½ the most common. Rods of such lengths are usually available in light, medium or heavy classes, so you rarely need a shorter or longer rod. Ultralight rods may be shorter, especially if you fish small, heavily wooded streams where a long rod is awkward. But the majority of all-purpose spinning rods will range from 6 to 7 ft. in length.

The kind of "action" a spinning rod has is important because it will determine the distance and accuracy of your casts and the weight of lures it will handle. Some rods have a fast tip action in which only a short section of the tip of the rod bends or flexes. Other rods bend along a greater length, and these are often very satisfactory to use since they are easier to cast with, handle lighter lures and are fun to play a fish on. Most of the regular fresh-water spinning rods are designed to handle a certain range of lure weights and aren't too good for casting lures that are too light or too heavy.

In recent years, however, the so-called "progressive-taper" rods have been developed to handle a wide range of lures. If you use light lures only, the extreme sensitive tip section will bend during the cast. If you change to a heavier lure, more of the rod is brought into play and it bends farther down toward the butt. Then if you change to a still heavier lure, the full length of the rod is brought into play and it curves almost to the butt. With such an action in a spinning rod you can handle a wider range of lures than with other rods. In other words, whereas in former years you needed two or three rods to handle most of the fresh-water lures made, now you can often get a single rod to do this work.

You hear a lot about "balanced" tackle. This merely means that the rod, reel and line are suited to each other and work well in combination. However, one man's idea of balanced tackle may not appeal to another. Many expert anglers who know what they are doing will use unbalanced tackle for certain kinds of fishing and under certain conditions. For example, you may want to use a fresh-water spin rod to cast light lures. Yet you expect to hook a big fish which will run off a lot of line. To have enough line on their reels of sufficient strength or to make long casts, some anglers use the smaller salt-water reels with the fresh-water rod. Technically speaking, this isn't a balanced outfit, but it's practical for the fishing being done. But, in general, for efficient casting and use, it is better to stick to a balanced outfit.

A beginner can go wrong when buying a separate rod, reel, line or lures and end up with an outfit unsuited for fishing. To play safe, it pays to ask the advice of an experienced spin angler in selecting the outfit. If you know a fishing-tackle dealer who knows his tackle, he'll advise you as to the right combination.

You can also buy one of those spinning kits where the rod, reel, line and lures are sold in one package. Here the manufacturer has selected the right rod, reel and line to make up a balanced outfit. Some lures are usually included, too. You can't go wrong if you buy one of these, especially one of the moderately priced or more expensive kits. It is the safest way for a beginner to buy a spinning outfit blind through the mail.

5

Salt-water Spinning Rods

It wasn't too many years ago that the angler who wanted to use spinning tackle in salt water was limited to either fresh-water rods or to a small selection of salt-water models. Today the picture is completely different, with a wide variety of salt-water spinning rods on the market. You can find a salt-water spinning rod to take care of almost any kind of fishing in the ocean that you can imagine.

As with fresh-water rods, hollow-glass rods are the first choice for salt-water spinning. Solid-glass rods have their uses for bottom fishing, jigging and trolling, but for casting and all-around use you can't beat hollow glass.

When it comes to salt-water rods, all the metal fittings and parts, such as reel seats, ferrules and guides, should be made of noncorrosive materials. The reel seat should be the locking-screw type which holds the reel securely in place. When you buy a salt-water spinning rod make sure that the reel will fit the reel seat on your rod. There are many different kinds of reels on the market and they often vary in the size and thickness of the reel foot. So check the fit before you buy any rod.

The guides on salt-water spinning rods should be wrapped on firmly with thread and have plenty of varnish. You can easily test this in a store by grabbing each guide and shaking it to see if it's loose. A little movement can't be avoided, but if they are too loose they may get out of line later. The guides on salt-water rods take more wear than those on fresh-water rods, especially the tip guide, where the reeling in of heavy lures and sinkers and playing of big fish soon cuts grooves in soft metal. Make sure that they are of the hardest metal.

When using a big, open-spool spinning reel, the first gathering guide should be very large. These big salt-water reels have large diameter spools, and if the guides are too small you lose distance on your casts. The first guide nearest the reel is usually of extra-large diameter, and on some of the longer, heavier salt-water spinning rods used in surf fishing may be $2\frac{1}{2}$ to 3 in. in diameter. The guides should graduate in size progressively to smaller ones toward the tip. There should be enough guides to distribute the strain evenly along the entire length of the rod.

We can divide salt-water spinning rods into three major classes: light, medium and heavy. The light salt-water spin rods are very similar to the heavy fresh-water models. In fact, you can use your heavy fresh-water rod for light salt-water fishing. The guides on a light salt-water rod may be a bit larger and heavier than those found on fresh-water rods because of the larger diameter spools on most salt-water reels. Another difference is that the lower grip or handle is often longer on the salt-water rod. This is a big aid in working lures such as surface plugs and jigs. The handle can rest against your forearm, saving the wrist. A longer handle is also less tiring when fighting a fish for any length of time. You can rest it against your groin or in a rod belt.

A light salt-water spinning rod should be light enough and short enough to cast with one hand. This means that the 6, $6\frac{1}{2}$ and 7-ft. lengths are best for this work. Some of the rods in this class will handle lures up to $1\frac{1}{2}$ oz., but most of them are designed to cast lures up to an ounce or so. However, they can cast light lures down to $\frac{3}{8}$ oz. with thin lines. This makes such a rod a versatile tool. Usually you will use lines testing 6, 8 or 10 lbs., depending on the weight of the lures cast and the size of the fish being sought.

The light spinning rod is ideal for boat fishing in bays, sounds, rivers and other shallow waters. It can also be used from shore in the quieter waters and makes a good rod for wading and fishing in Florida, the Bahamas, the Gulf of Mexico and other shallow waters and protected waters. For such fish as small striped bass, bluefish, weakfish or sea trout, snook, channel bass, steelhead and small salmon, the light rod is sporty and effective. It also makes a good jigging rod with bucktail or nylon jigs or small diamond jigs for the smaller fish.

Although used mainly for casting artificial lures, the light rod can also be used for bottom fishing in shallow water where currents aren't too strong. (You can't use sinkers much heavier than 2 oz.) The light rod can also be used for light trolling. The best reels to use with the light rods are the fresh-water models or smaller salt-water types.

The medium salt-water rods run from about 7 to 10 ft. in overall length. These rods have a butt or handle anywhere from 14 to 22 in. long and are cast with two hands. The shorter, lighter rods in this class make good boat rods and also shore-casting rods. The longer ones can be used for light surf fishing. In this class you'll find many of the steelhead and salmon rods used for drift fishing in the rivers. And the longer 9-ft. models are widely used for "mooching" in the Northwest for salmon. The medium-weight rods can usually handle up to $2\frac{1}{2}$ oz. and somewhat heavier sinkers. Lines testing from 10 to 20 lb. are usually used with these rods. This rod makes a good pier, bridge or jetty rod where long casts are not required and heavy lures or sinkers are not used. It can also be used for light trolling and bottom fishing with bait. If a man had to choose just one spinning rod for salt-water fishing, the medium rod is the most versatile.

The heavy rod can run from $8\frac{1}{2}$ on up to 14 ft. in length.

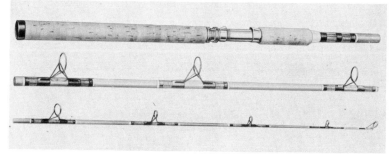

True Temper Montague rod is made in one piece and is 9 ft. long. It has a fast-tip action for heavy surf, pier and live-bait fishing.

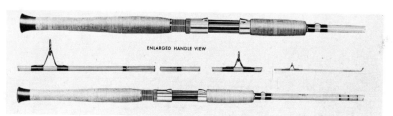

ENLARGED HANDLE VIEW

Wright & McGill "Granger" salt-water spinning rod comes in 7, 7½, and 8 ft. lengths.

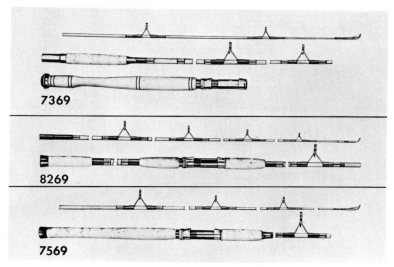

7369

8269

7569

South Bend "Sea Master" surf spinning rods are designed for medium and heavy action. They range from 8 to 9 feet in length.

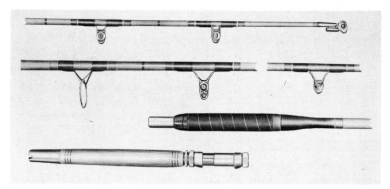

Continental-Alcedo big-game roller-guide rod. Designed for monster fishing when matched with the Alcedo Mark V Super spin reel.

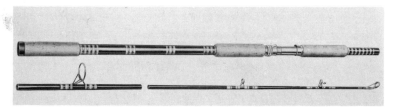

The Montague surf spinning rod comes in one piece 10½ ft. in over-all length.

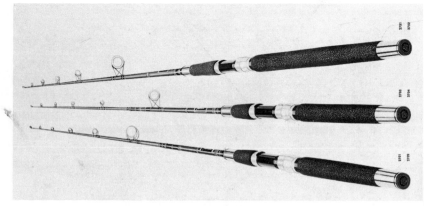

Garcia-Conolon "Custom" rods range in length from 6½ to 9 ft. to handle various salt-water-fishing conditions and lures from light to heavy.

Such rods are the most practical for most surf fishing along both the Atlantic and Pacific coasts. Such rods are capable of handling lures and sinkers up to 4 and 5 oz. and can be used for the heaviest fishing in the surf. Lines testing from 15 to 30 lbs. are used with these rods, which can cast great distances.

Although primarily a surf rod, the heavy spinning rod in the shorter and longer lengths can also be used from boats. On the West Coast, for example, the heavy spinning rods in lengths from 9 to 12 ft. are often used for "live-bait" and jig fishing from the Southern California party boats for albacore, yellowtail and small tuna.

In the heavy-spinning-rod class you'll also find the offshore spinning rods which are used in trolling for sailfish, marlin, tuna, swordfish and sharks. A special rod of this type, with roller guides and swiveling roller tip-top, has been made by the tackle division of the Continental Arms Corporation of New York. This rod also has a heavy-duty big-game locking reel seat and solid wood butt. It also has a slotted butt cap which fits into the gimbal of a fishing chair.

In general, the construction of these heavy spinning rods varies according to the manufacturer. Some have heavy, hardwood butts and heavy brass, chrome-plated reel seats. Others have lighter, hollow-glass butts with light aluminium reel seats and cork grips. This makes a somewhat lighter rod. For surf fishing a one-piece tip section fitted into a separate butt section makes the most convenient rod. Other rods are made in two pieces, with the ferrule about midway or near the butt. These are also convenient for traveling and storing. The strongest rods are those made from one-piece hollow-glass blanks with cork grips. These rods are also very light, but because of their length they are more of a problem when it comes to transporting or storing them. They must be carried outside the car on rod carriers and you can't hide them in a closet if they are very long.

The trend nowadays is toward longer spinning surf rods on

both the East and West Coasts. Surf rods running up to 10, 11 and 12 ft. in over-all length are very popular. The longer rods are better for all-around use and for fishing under different conditions. They make it easier to handle the casting of bait rigs that have long leaders. And they are also better when it comes to working certain lures and for fighting a fish. And when cast from the beach they often make it easier to obtain more distance.

The shorter surf rods have a place for fishing from jetties, breakwaters and rocky shores where you don't have to cast too far. They are also lighter and easier to handle in "squidding" with artificial lures, when you make repeated casts for hours at a time.

Nowadays you can find almost exactly the length and action you want in a salt-water spinning rod. And if you get one of the newer progressive-taper designs, you have a single rod which can be used for most surf-fishing conditions and areas. Such rods will handle a wide range of lure weights, so that you can cast light lures or heavy lures, as the need arises.

6

Spin-casting Rods and Reels

IN RECENT YEARS there has been a big boom in the popularity of the so-called "spin-cast" or "push-button" reels. These are the closed-faced reels mounted above the rod like a bait-casting reel. To cast with them, you simply push a button, begin your cast, then release the button to start the lure on its way. These reels are so easy to use that in many parts of the country they are out-selling all other types of fresh-water reels.

The spin-casting reel is almost foolproof and you rarely have trouble with the line tangling or uncoiling, as sometimes happens with the open-faced spinning reels. This is especially desirable when fishing on windy days or at night. The open-faced reels often offer trouble at such times, when the line tangles around the bail or the reel itself. Spin-casting reels are also accurate and faster to use than the open-faced reels. You can time the release of your lure to a split second when casting, and send it flying to the target with precision and speed.

One of the main disadvantages of the spin-casting reel is that it doesn't attain the distances, especially with light lures, that the open-faced reel does. You usually use at least a 4-lb. test line and mostly 6 or 8-lb. test lines with spin-casting reels. So these reels aren't exactly made for the ultralight angler who wants to use light lures and lines. If you like to use the lightest lines and lures and want to cast the maximum distance, stay with the open-faced spinning reel. But for the average man, woman or child who wants an all-around fresh-water fishing outfit, the spin-casting reel is ideal.

Spin-casting reels can also be used on the regular bait-casting rods in a pinch. However, some bait-casting rods may be too stiff or too short for such use. So it's safer to buy a special spin-casting rod. More and more companies are making such rods for use with both spin-casting and bait-casting rods.

The main differences between a spin-casting rod and a bait-casting rod are the length, action, and type and size of the guides. In general, the bait-casting rods are somewhat shorter, stiffer in action, and have smaller guides. By comparison, spin-casting rods are longer, have a more limber action and larger guides.

Spin-casting rods are made in various types of actions and lengths. Some rod manufacturers list four different actions: extra-light, light, medium and heavy. Others make the spin-casting rods in only two or three actions. Some of the lighter rods can be used with 4-lb. test line to cast lures as light as $\frac{1}{8}$ oz. Heavy-action rods can handle lures up to one ounce or so, but the majority of spin-casting rods are made to handle lures weighing from $\frac{1}{4}$ to $\frac{5}{8}$ oz.

The length of the spin-casting rod you use will depend on your personal preference. Most such rods come in 6, $6\frac{1}{2}$ and 7 ft. over-all length. There are also longer and somewhat heavier rods, for specialized fishing, which may run up to 8 ft. in length. But for most of your fishing you'll find that the 6 or $6\frac{1}{2}$-ft. rod will be adequate. Such rods are usually made in two sections, with the ferrule in the middle. But they can also be obtained in three sections, with a detachable handle and two tip sections. Other spin-casting rods are made with long one-piece tips and detachable handles. Still other special spin-casting rods are made in four sections, for easy packing in a small space.

*Garcia Abu-Matic 140 is a push-button reel with a star drag,
synchro-drag, and holds 125yds. of 8-lb. test line*

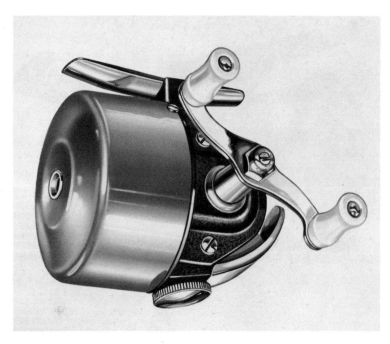

Plueger "Galaxie" spin-casting reel is designed for medium-duty fishing. It comes filled with 100yds. of 10-lb. test line.

The reel seat on most spin-casting rods is the same offset type found on most bait-casting rods. These seats are usually made from die-cast aluminium or other metals and plastics. The reel seat on such rods should lock a spin-casting reel securely in place. The grips and handles are made of cork or plastic.

The guides on a spin-casting rod are smaller than those found on rods used with open-faced spinning reels, but they are somewhat larger than those found on a true bait-casting rod. However, as stated before, many manufacturers are now making the same rod for use with both spin-casting and bait-casting reels. Therefore the size of the guides used will work well with either type of reel. The great majority of spin-casting rods are made from hollow- or tubular-glass blanks. These have the best action for all-around spin-casting. Some of the cheapest rods are made from solid glass; and while inferior in action and heavier than hollow glass, such rods are extremely strong and are suitable for rough fishing or for youngsters.

The closed-faced spin-casting reel is very similar to the closed-faced spinning reel covered previously. But instead of hanging below the rod as the other spinning reels do, the spin-casting reel is mounted above the rod. However, the construction and mechanical operation of the spin-casting reel is similar to the type which hangs below the rod.

The spin-casting reel also has a cone-shaped face in front of the reel. The line comes out of a small hole and loses most of its swirl, thus enabling this reel to be used with rods having small guides. The hole through which the line comes out is lined with a smooth, hard metal ring, so that the line doesn't wear. The cone in front of the reel can usually be removed quickly and easily on most of the reels, for quick access to the line on the spool.

Most of the spin-casting reels also have a thumb button or trigger, which is pushed and held down when ready to cast. Then, when the lure is released, the thumb is lifted off the button. On many of the reels you can also press on the button lightly, feathering it while the lure is in flight to control or slow down its speed. To stop the cast, you can press down firmly on the button.

Spin-casting reels also have an antireverse which prevents the handle from turning backward. On some reels this consists of a knurled ring or button which can be turned to the "on" or "off" position, as required. But many other spin-casting reels are made with a permanent antireverse which stays on at all times.

The brakes or drags found on most spin-casting reels are generally smooth and efficient. Some earlier models gave trouble in this respect if the drag was uneven or if the line should bind and break. Different makes have different types of drags and methods of drag adjustment. Most of the spin-casting reels have a knob or lever, which is moved to increase or decrease the drag tension. Some are numbered, so that the drag can be set at a predetermined tension. Other reels have star-drags such as those found on conventional salt-water reels.

The spools on spin-casting reels are much narrower than those found on open-faced spinning reels. This solves the problem of the line piling up unevenly in the front or back of the spool, as often happens with the wider open-faced spinning reels. However, the narrow spool also creates another problem in some reels by causing the parallel-wound line to bury itself under the other strands of line under tension such as occurs when the angler plays a fish or pulls on the line when it gets fouled or caught. This buried line must be worked free before another cast can be made. This problem has been remedied in later models, which cross-wind the line to overcome this tendency.

The line pick-up, which catches the line during the retrieve, should be made of some hard substance such as Carboloy. There is a lot of wear and friction at this point, and a soft metal will become grooved and eventually damage the line. Some of the earlier models of spin-casting reels also twisted the line badly

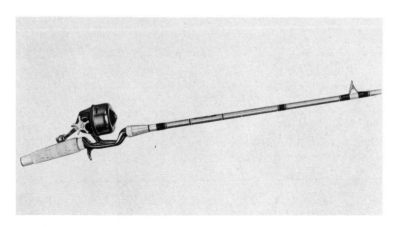

This Garcia spin-casting rod and reel make a good combination. Spin-casting rods are very similar to bait-casting rods except that they are usually a little longer and can cast lighter lures. They also have somewhat larger guides.

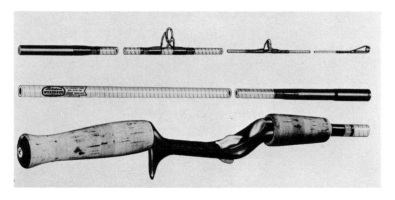

Shakespeare push-button Wonderod comes in two pieces and in 6 and 6½ ft. lengths.

Heddon Scandia Mark IV spin-casting reel features audio-touch control which enables a caster to hear the degree of thumbing pressure being applied.

Wright & McGill spin-cast reel has push button, and mounts above the rod.

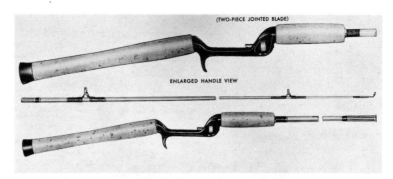

Wright & McGill "Granger" special-duty spin-casting rod is 8 ft. long and can be used for heavy fresh-water or light salt-water spin casting.

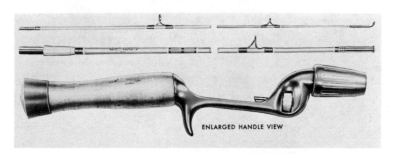

Wright & McGill "Champion" spin-casting rod comes in 6, 6½, and 7 ft. lengths. It is made in two pieces, with detachable handle.

when it was rewound on the spool. This twisting has been eliminated on many of the later models.

Most spin-casting reels have interchangeable spools, which can be removed and replaced by other spools filled with new lines or with lines of different tests. Most of the spin-casting reels come from the factory filled with 6 or 8-lb. test monofilament line. Some fresh-water models can also be used with lines testing 10, 12 or 15 lbs. There are also a few special heavy-duty fresh-water and salt-water spin-casting reels which can be used with heavier lines up to 20-lb. test. For most fresh-water fishing, lines testing 6 or 8 lbs. are sufficient. The average spin-casting reel will hold anywhere from 80 to 150 yds. of line, depending on the pound test. This is more than enough for fresh-water fishing.

Spin-casting reels are usually made of light metals such as aluminium alloys, which are anodized or satin-chromed to protect them. However, more and more plastics are also being utilized to make such reels.

The majority of spin-casting reels are made with a right-handed crank or handle. In other words, you're supposed to cast with your right hand, then transfer the rod and reel to your left hand and turn the reel handle with your right hand. However, some companies also make spin-casting reels with a left-hand crank, for retrieving with your left hand, like most open-faced spinning reels. Other spin-casting reels can be changed so that the handle is either on the left- or right-hand side. Whichever reel you get depends on your own habits and personal preference. If you have used a bait-casting or surf-casting conventional revolving-spool reel most of your life, you'll find the right-hand crank more familiar. If you started fishing with an open-faced spinning reel, you'll probably find the left-hand crank the more familiar. That way you don't have to learn or unlearn any hand movements. But it really doesn't take very long to get used to a new reel if you cast and fish with it often enough.

The spin-casting reel has made casting so simple that instead of spending hours, days or weeks practicing how to cast you can go out on the first day and concentrate on catching fish. Of course, even with the spin-casting reel you must practice and do quite a bit of casting before you become accurate. But in most fishing waters such accuracy is not required. As long as the lure or bait lands within a few feet of the target the lack of greater accuracy usually doesn't make too much difference in open waters. It's mainly when you are casting toward shore or toward a rock, log or tree stump and want the lure to land on a very small target that you need accuracy.

Spin-casting reels are so easy to use and so foolproof that they make ideal tools for the casual or beginning angler. You'll find this the best reel to get if you are buying your first fishing tackle. Even expert anglers like to use them at night, when other reels are apt to give trouble.

7

Spinning Lines

IT IS DOUBTFUL whether spinning would have reached its present popularity without the rapid development of the modern spinning line. Most of the earlier lines used in spin fishing, such as cotton, linen, silk and Japanese gut, were never too good, and it was only when DuPont came out with nylon that the big improvement began.

The first lines made in this country especially for spinning were mostly of braided nylon and were stiff and thick in diameter. They have been improved considerably since then. When dacron was developed, spinning lines were made from this material, and such lines are usually preferred over braided nylon for spinning. They are thin in diameter, have less stretch and cast well.

Either braided nylon or dacron lines have their limited uses. When fishing with bass bugs, popping plugs or similar surface lures, where you reel with jerks, pauses and even complete stops as the lure lies on the surface without moving, the braided lines often give less trouble than other types. They spool somewhat better on the reel than monofilament lines. Braided lines also stay on the spool and do not jump off in coils or bunches. But braided nylon or dacron lines are visible in the water and monofilament leaders must be used ahead of the line for best results. In the heavier tests, such as those used for surf fishing or bottom fishing around rocks, reefs and coral, braided lines do not stand up as well as monofilament. They also tend to fray and wear from continuous casting and friction against the guides.

So for all-around use you can't beat the monofilament spinning lines. Today you'll find most fresh- and salt-water anglers using monofilament. In this country most monofilament lines are made from DuPont nylon, which is processed, labeled and dyed by various fishing-line manufacturers under different trade names. Of course, each manufacturer claims his product is superior, and gives reasons. Although made from the same basic raw material, they do vary somewhat in strength for a given diameter, stretch, limpness, hardness, softness, etc.

There are also imported monofilament lines, such as Platyl, and this line is very popular with many fresh- and salt-water fishermen. It is limp and thin, has very little stretch and has been improved in recent years.

DuPont also makes a monofilament called "Stren," which has a smaller diameter than the original nylon monofilament and is also limper and has less stretch. It comes in tests from 2 to 30 lbs. and is pale gun-metal in color, which is almost invisible in water.

Which line you get will depend, of course, on what kind of fishing you do most of the time. Try a few different brands and types until you find one which suits you. You can't go wrong with any of the reputable manufacturers' standard brands described in these pages. Stay away from "bargain" lines and other lines marketed by firms not associated with the fishing industry.

Spinning lines, both braided and monofilament, come dyed in different colors. A colorless or light-blue, green or gray line is best for most fishing conditions. But there isn't too much harm in using other colors, such as light-brown, pink or violet. Spinning lines are so thin that it is doubtful whether a fish can pick up the color of a line. Reflections or glint is another matter. Most early spin lines had a high-gloss finish, which made a line appear thicker than it actually was. This could scare a wary fish under certain light and water conditions. As a result, some line manufacturers are now turning out lines with dull finishes. One of the best non-reflective lines on the market is "Tortue" which is distributed in this country by Elegante Imports.

The size of the line you buy will depend on several factors: the weight of the lures you cast, the weight and stiffness of the rod, where you intend to fish, the kind and size of fish you intend to catch and whether you are a novice or an expert.

Let's take these one by one, and see how they affect the choice of the line strength. Ultralight lines, testing from $\frac{1}{2}$ lb. to 3 lbs. or so, must be used with the ultralight rods made for this fishing. You can't use them on heavier or stiffer rods without breaking them under the slightest strain. If you are using the light fresh-water lures running from $\frac{1}{16}$ to $\frac{1}{4}$ oz. in weight you can't go much heavier than 3 or 4 lbs. in lines and cast them any distance. For the average weight of spinning lures, running from $\frac{1}{8}$ to $\frac{1}{2}$ oz., you can use 4 or 6-lb. test lines. If you plan to use heavier lures from $\frac{1}{2}$ to 1 oz. in weight, you can go to 8 or 10 lb. test lines. For the heaviest fresh-water fishing for such fish as pike, muskies, lake trout, carp, catfish and similar heavyweights, you may need lines testing from 10 to 20 lbs. under certain conditions and in many areas.

In salt-water fishing, 6 or 8-lb. test lines can be used for light fishing or casting with a one-hand spinning rod. For heavier salt-water spinning rods and light surf fishing, you may use lines testing 10, 12 and 15 lbs. For heavier boat and surf fishing, you may need lines testing from 15 to 20 lbs. And for the heaviest surf-fishing conditions and offshore fishing, lines from 20 to 40-lb. test may be used. Nowadays, with monofilaments becoming thinner and thinner and more and more dependable and limper, you can use such heavy tests and get enough line on the reel.

The rod action also governs the size of the line used. A long, limber rod will take the shock of casting and playing a fish much better than a shorter, stiffer rod. So you can use lighter lines with the lighter, limper rods.

In open waters where a fish is allowed to run freely, you can land lunkers on light lines. But in snag-infested waters with weeds, stumps, logs, rocks, etc., you need heavier lines to slow down or turn a fish away. Likewise, in surf fishing along open beaches with no obstructions, you can get away with using lighter lines than you can along rocky shores, around piles, jetties or breakwaters. In the open ocean you can land the big sailfish and smaller marlins with fairly light lines if you have someone who knows how to handle the boat. Strong surf and currents also demand stronger lines.

In trolling you use heavier lines than when casting, first, because, in casting, the lighter lines give you more distance, and second, because trolling places a heavier strain on a line. The fish is hooked when the boat is moving and the sudden shock can snap a light line. Also you often get hung up in sunken trees, logs, weeds and rocks, and this also strains the lines.

The same thing is true if you use your spinning outfit for bottom fishing in salt water. Here you may have the line rub against rocks, piles, mussels or barnacles, or you may get tangled around some obstruction. To break free without losing the rig, hook and bait, you need a pretty strong line.

Salt-water fishing in general places more strain on lines and there's more wear and tear from various sources. First, you are never sure just what you may hook. You may be fishing for small fish weighing a few pounds when suddenly a "monster" close to a hundred pounds or more may take hold. Then you also have to contend with strong tides, currents, surf, heavier lures and sinkers, which all place a strain on the line.

When fishing from a bridge, pier or shore, where you may have to lift fish any distance, you need stronger lines than when fishing from a boat or at the same level as the water, where a net or gaff can be used. Even a small fish of only a few pounds com-

Garcia Platyl monofilament comes in various tests from 1 to 50 lbs. It is thin in diameter, supple and strong.

Spinning lines now come in various diameters, colors and degrees of limpness.

Spinning lines come in coils like this or on spools, and are usually connected, so that any length can be obtained.

bined with the weight of the sinker can place a heavy strain on the line.

The skill of the angler also determines line strength. A beginner is better off with a slightly stronger line until he learns how to cast and play a fish. An expert with a light outfit and line can make "stunt" catches which a beginner shouldn't even attempt. It takes quite a bit of experience to judge just how much strain your line will take before popping. But even the experts lose some nice fish with spinning tackle because of broken lines. If you want the most sport and fun you have to expect that. It must be remembered that spinning tackle is no cure-all or answer to all your fishing needs. There are times when it is more sensible to use another type of tackle.

Because you can change spools on most spinning reels so easily many anglers carry one or two extra spools filled with different-sized lines. Then they are ready for most fishing conditions.

After you buy your line you will have to put it on the reel. A few open-spool reels come with the spool filled at the factory. And most closed-spool and spin-casting-type reels come with filled spools. If you have to fill a reel spool on an open-faced spinning reel you can often have it done at the tackle store where you buy the reel. Many of these places have line-winders and will fill the spool on the reel and any extra spools you want. They often sell the line from bulk spools cheaper than you can buy it on small spools.

If you must spool the line on the reel yourself follow the directions in the instruction booklet supplied with the spinning reel. There are so many different types of spinning reels on the market now that it is difficult to give one method of spooling lines that will apply to all reels. One method which usually works with most reels is to tie your line to the reel spool and wind it on with the reel handle. The line spool should revolve around a pencil or rod. Tension should be applied by having someone hold the line spool and press against the sides. If you are alone you can put the pencil or rod in a vise or some other setup that will hold it in place and run the line through your fingers while you reel with the other hand. The line should be packed fairly tight but not too tight.

The amount of line you put on the reel is important. For most fresh-water fishing you rarely need more than 100 yds. of line. The rest underneath can be backing of old braided nylon or some other line. However, there should be enough line to fill the reel spool almost to the lip or flange. Overfilling will cause the line to fly off in loops or coils and will cause snarls. If you haven't enough line on the reel spool you'll cut down your casting distance, since there is too much friction when the line tries to jump the flange on the spool.

For ordinary salt-water fishing and surf fishing 200 to 350 yds. of line is usually enough. If long casts are made and big fish are expected in the surf the larger reels holding 300 to 400 yds. are best. And, of course, for offshore fishing, where you may hook sailfish, marlin or other big fish, you may need even more line. In any of this heavy fishing in the surf or offshore it's a good idea to fill the entire spool with line. Heavy backing line will fill the reel spool too quickly, leaving little room for the actual fishing or casting line. Besides, a line in one piece is always stronger than one with knots in it.

8

How to Cast

EARLY IN THIS BOOK I said that spin casting is easy and that even a beginner can learn how to cast in a short time. That's still true; but you should get off to a good start either by having an expert caster show you the first basic steps or by studying written instructions carefully and then teaching yourself. This section will describe the various casting procedures. It's important to get off to a good start, so that you don't pick up bad habits that will be difficult to change later on.

First, of course, you have to set up the rod and reel for casting. With rods which have fixed-locking reel seats you have to fasten the reel in that spot. With sliding retaining rings you fasten the reel anywhere along the handle that feels comfortable. Most experienced anglers like to fasten the reel as far up the cork handle as possible. This usually feels best and gives you a longer cork handle below, which provides leverage for working lures and fighting a fish. The retaining rings should fit tight, so that the reel doesn't wobble. If it doesn't feel secure you can get some adhesive or plastic tape and wind it around the reel foot and the rings. Make sure that the reel spool lines up directly opposite the guides on the rod.

Most fresh-water spin casting is done by holding the rod with

81

the right hand directly above the reel. The reel hangs below the handle. The thumb rests on top of the cork handle, while two fingers are below in front of the reel stem and the other two fingers are behind this support. However, this may vary with the angler. Some like three fingers in front of the reel stem. In some closed-spool reels the whole hand is in front of the reel.

The basic spin cast is the overhead cast. The lure or casting weight should hang about 6 in. or so from the tip of the rod. The first step with an open-faced reel is to move the pick-up device into casting position. With a manual type reel you bring the line roller to the top so that you can pick up the line with the index finger of your right hand. Then the line roller is moved out of the way, so that it rests at the bottom of the reel. With reels that have finger pick-ups you do the same thing, turning the handle so that the line can be grabbed with the index finger. Then back the handle so that the finger pick-up moves to the bottom of the reel, after which you push the finger or arm down and away from the reel spool.

For this practice casting the antireverse should be in the "off" position. When using the full bail pick-up reel you turn the handle until the line roller is on top, permitting you to grab the line with your index finger. Then back off the reel handle so that the line is free from the roller. Finally, using your left hand, push the wire bail down until it is in casting position at the bottom of the reel.

When your reel is ready to cast, rest the line on the ball of your index finger. Next hold the rod in front of you at about the 10-o'clock position. Point it at the target. Now bring the rod back fast toward you so that the tip points up into the air above your head at about the 12-o'clock position. Without a pause, immediately start the rod tip forward. This should be a fast snap. As the rod moves forward it will bend into an arc under the weight of the lure. When it reaches the 10-o'clock position again, the index finger releases the line and the lure shoots out

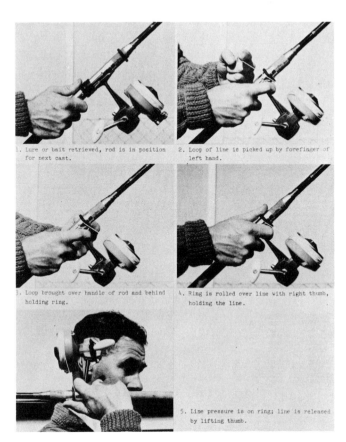

1. Lure or bait retrieved, rod is in position for next cast.

2. Loop of line is picked up by forefinger of left hand.

3. Loop brought over handle of rod and behind holding ring.

4. Ring is rolled over line with right thumb, holding the line.

5. Line pressure is on ring; line is released by lifting thumb.

True Temper medium- and heavy-duty salt-water rods are now equipped with a holding ring which prevents wear, tear and cuts on the index finger when casting.

in front of you at a fast speed. When it reaches the target or just above it you drop your index finger to the lip of the spool to stop the cast. You can also stop the cast by turning the handle on an automatic pick-up reel.

If your lure goes high into the air it means that you released the line too soon. If it drops at your feet or a short distance away it means you released the line too late. This will take a bit of practice before you get the right timing. A good way to get the feel of the rod and lure is to have the line on your index finger ready to cast, then wave the rod back and forth from the 10-o'clock to the 12-o'clock position without releasing the line from your index finger. Just go through the motions, waving it back and forth. You will feel the rod flexing under the weight of the lure. Then after a minute or two of this, try releasing the lure at the right moment.

This is the basic overhead cast. Once you learn this well, the other casts will be easy. The overhead cast is the most accurate and will drop your lure in a straight line in front of you. In actual fishing, however, the lure doesn't have to hit a small target most of the time. Many anglers hold the rod a bit to the right side so that it doesn't travel exactly over their head.

In the side cast the rod travels almost parallel to the ground or water. It is not as accurate as the overhead cast but is useful for casting under overhanging trees or into a strong wind. The lure travels low and you get more distance against the wind.

Another cast which will enable you to fish from shore in heavy brush and woods is the bow-and-arrow cast. Here you let the lure hang down about half the length of the rod. Then you grab the lure carefully with your left fingers at the bend of the hook (not ahead of the points) and pull back until the rod flexes into a bow. The rod can be bent up or down; it doesn't make much difference. Now aim toward your target. Then release the lure with your left hand and let the line slip off your index finger.

Another cast also used in heavy brush is the lariat or circle cast. Here the lure dangles from the rod tip about a foot or so and you twirl it around in a circle in front of you. Then as it reaches a good speed you release the line and the lure shoots out to one side. To cast in the opposite direction you twirl the rod in the other direction.

There are a few other casts, but the ones mentioned will take care of most fishing situations. You'll pick up others as you go along. In the beginning it pays to try for accuracy and not distance. After you learn how to cast you can try for distance.

There's usually a maximum distance you can reach with a given line and lure. If you want to cast farther you change to a lighter line or heavier lure, or both. A longer rod also helps attain a bit more distance under certain conditions. The type of lure used also affects your casting and the distance you reach. With large, bulky lures, such as bass bugs, big plugs, big spinners and spoons, you don't get as much distance as with the smaller, compact lures. They offer too much wind resistance. However, except for large rivers and salt-water fishing such as surf fishing, distance is rarely required to catch fish. Most of your fish in fresh water will be caught within the 100-ft. mark.

When casting with closed-spool-type reels or spin-casting reels you go through the same motions as above. The only thing that may differ is the release of the line, depending on the model of reel you are using. On some closed-spool reels that hang under the rod you can hold the line on your index finger or against the cork handle. Most spin-casting reels have some kind of trigger or button which is held down by the thumb. This locks the line and lure in place, so that it doesn't slide down. Then as the cast is completed you release the button freeing the line and sending the lure on its way. On most spin-casting reels you can stop the cast by pressing the button. Then you simply turn the handle forward to catch the line again, so that it can be retrieved. The clerk in any store where you buy the reel will show you how it operates. You can also get more information by reading the booklet or instruction sheet for that particular reel.

With the heaviest fresh-water rods and most salt-water rods you must use two hands for casting. The cork handle or butt on these rods is longer, in order to accommodate two hands, and may range from 15 to 30 in. in length. With the lighter salt-water one-handed rods the casting procedure is exactly the same as with the one-hand fresh-water spinning rods. However, they are usually heavier and so are the lures, and you don't get the same speed or snap with them, and your wrist and arm tire sooner.

With the two-hand salt-water rod you place your right hand above the reel the same way as with the fresh-water rod described earlier. But you then take your left hand and grasp the end of the butt. You release the line from the pick-up and hold it with your index finger, as in fresh-water casting. To make the overhead cast you go through the same motions as with the one-hand fresh-water rod except that you can bring the rod a bit lower in front of you, say slightly above the 9-o'clock position. Then bring it back over your head and let it drop behind you to about the 1-o'clock position. Then, as the lure bends the rod into a big arc, you start the forward cast by pushing with your right hand and pulling back with your left. This is done in a continuous quick snap. When the rod reaches the 10-o'clock position in front of you, let go the line and the lure will sail out a great distance. Timing here is just as important as in fresh-water casting, and will come with practice.

The other method used is similar to surf casting with the conventional surf rod. Here you hold the rod almost parallel to the ground behind you. Then with a fast forward snap you bring the rod over your head in front of you and at about the 10-o'clock position release the line from your finger. This cast is best with the heavier, longer surf spinning rods and heavy lures.

There are other casts which can be used with the two-hand salt-water spinning rods. The side cast is used against a strong

wind. When fishing from bridges or piers you often point the rod
down toward the water and then flip it out quickly away from
the structure. When in a boat or other spot where space and
movement is limited you can often do a modified version of the
overhead cast by holding the rod up and slightly in front of you.
Then you bring it back and forward very quickly in a short
radius, to snap the lure out.

When casting with heavy surf rods and heavy lures you can
cut your index finger with the line or make it tender and sore.
The True Temper Corporation recently announced a new rod
with a holding ring mounted on the handle of the rod just ahead
of the reel seat, intended to prevent such soreness. The fisherman,
after the retrieve, takes a loop of line with his left hand, brings
it over the rod handle and behind the ring and rolls the ring over
the line with his right thumb. On the back cast all the pressure of
the mono line is transferred to the holding ring, thus saving wear,
tear and cuts on the index finger. The line is released for the
cats by merely lifting the thumb from the holding ring. Other
companies have come out with similar devices to hold the line
while casting.

If you can, practice casting in a nearby lake or river or in the
ocean. This approximates actual fishing conditions and the line
is taut and spools evenly and under the proper tension. When
practicing on land you get slack line and loose coils, and can ruin
a good spinning line reeling it across stones, gravel, cement and
abrasive surfaces. If you must cast on land, select a lawn. For
dry-land practice casting you need one of the rubber practice
weights or a small block of wood with a screw eye in it.

Casting is not much of a problem in spinning, and most anglers
soon learn how to get the lure out a considerable distance with
fair accuracy. Casting alone won't make you a good angler. It
helps, but there are a lot of other things you must know about
baits and lures, how to use them, where to find fish and how to fish
In the long run these are more important than casting ability.

9

Terminal Tackle

THE THIN LINES used in spin fishing are a great advantage when it comes to casting. You get plenty of distance with even light lures and they also play a big part in fooling wary fish. But these same lines present a disadvantage when it comes to wear and tear on the first few feet. Constant casting of lures often weakens the line where it rubs against the tip guide, and if too heavy a lure is used the shock of casting may break the line. The thin lines also can't take much rubbing against rocks, logs, coral, mussels, barnacles and similar obstructions. Then there's the strain of landing a fish near a boat or shore. You may have to hold him from running around the motor or propeller or you may have to partially drag him in shallow water or on the ground. In some spots you may even have to lift a small fish a short distance. In surf fishing you may have to fight the current, surf, waves and undertow when beaching a fish. Then there's the problem of sharp-toothed or gill-plated fish that can cut a line. All these things add up to wear or strain on the thin spinning lines. So spinning anglers are making use of various kinds of leaders to take some of the wear and tear off the lines.

In fishing in fresh water that is open and has no obstructions leaders are often not necessary. In fact, when fishing trout streams or clear waters with wary fish, leaders may cut down the number of strikes you get.

If you do require a leader the simplest one to use is another short length of nylon monofilament a few pounds stronger than your main fishing line. For best results such a leader should be long enough to leave a few turns of the leader on the reel spool when your lure is ready to cast. This is especially important in salt-water fishing, where heavy lures will break light lines or cut your forefinger. The length of your leader will depend on the length of your rod and the distance your lure hangs from the rod tip. It will vary, but as long as you have a few turns of leader on your reel spool the strain is off your line.

There are several knots which can be used to attach the leader to the line. One of the most widely used is the blood knot. To tie it, first lap the ends of the lines or leader and line to be tied. Then twist one around the other to make at least five turns. Next place one end between the strands and hold them together between your thumb and forefinger. Then wind the other end around the line or leader for the same number of turns in the opposite direction. Finally, you pull on the two ends to draw the turns closer together. When they bunch up, pull tight on the ends to make the knot as small as possible. Then clip off the ends close to the knot. (See illustration.) This knot is best when the difference between the line and leader aren't too great.

If there's a great variation in the thickness of the line and leader the double thumb or overhand knot is a good one to use. Here you merely lap the ends of the line and leader and then tie the thumb knot twice, as shown in the illustration.

The same double thumb knot can also be used to tie a quick loop on the end of a line or leader. Another good knot for tying a loop on the end of a line or leader is the perfection loop. Both these knots are illustrated so that you can learn to tie them easily.

One knot every spinning fisherman should know is the

improved clinch knot used to tie a leader or line to a hook, fly, lure, swivel or snap. To tie it, you run about three inches or a bit more of the end of the line or leader through the eye of the hook, lure or swivel. Then double it back and twist it around the leader or line for at least five turns. Next put the end through the opening next to the hook eye. At this point it can be tightened and will make an ordinary clinch knot. But for added security run the end of the leader or line through the big opening. Then pull on the end of the leader and slide the turns toward the eye of the hook or lure to tighten it. Then clip off the end. (See illustration.)

Nylon monofilament has a tendency to slip if not properly tied, so care must be taken in tightening the knots. After the knot is formed it should be pulled up slowly. Then it should be pulled tight. After the knot is tied do not clip off the end very short, except when necessary, such as in joining the line and leader. Here, in order for the line to move freely from the reel and through the guides, the ends must be clipped short. For added safety some anglers burn the end of the line or leader with a lighted cigarette after the knot is tied. This forms a small ball which makes it less likely that the knot will untie.

Various kinds of snaps, swivels and other connections are required at times in fresh- or salt-water spin fishing. When fishing trout streams or clear lakes for wary fish it is often best to tie the leader directly to the lure. However, if you plan to use many different kinds of lures this can be a time-consuming nuisance. Most spin anglers fishing the larger streams, lakes and salt water use some kind of snap or snap-swivel for changing the lures quickly. Several different types are on the market. One of the best snaps or snap-swivels made is the stainless steel snap designed by Ed Hatch of Pompanette Products. They are made in various sizes and tests, from tiny fresh-water snaps to giant tuna snaps.

The Art Wire and Stamping Company also makes different kinds of snaps and snap-swivels under the brand names of "Luxon" and "Kelux," which can be used in spinning.

Other terminal gear often used for trolling includes special trolling leads and keel swivels which add weight so that the lures travel down deep where the fish are. There are various sizes and weights which can be used for fresh and salt-water trolling with spinning rods.

Frankly, the less hardware you use when spinning the better results you get. Yet there are times when you can't avoid using such snaps, swivels and weights. The next best thing to do is to use the lightest and smallest sizes you can.

Wire leaders are not often required in fresh-water fishing except when fishing for such species as pike and muskellunge. Here a leader up to 30 in. may be needed when trolling and one somewhat shorter when casting.

In salt-water fishing you often need wire leaders on your lures or hooks, not only because of such sharp-toothed fish as bluefish and barracuda but also because the fins and gill covers of many salt-water fish will quickly cut a nylon leader.

Such wire leaders will, of course, vary with the type of fish you are seeking and the kind of fishing you are doing. Small, short ones are often permanently attached to jigs, metal squids, plugs and other lures. These are often no more than 6 or 8 in. long, so that they can be carried in a tackle box or small bag easily. One end has a small eye or loop to which the snap on the end of the leader is attached. The other end of the wire leader is permanently attached to the lure. (See Illustration.) For light spinning the shorter leaders of fine wire are best. For surf fishing you may use somewhat longer ones running about 8 or 10 in. in length.

When trolling for the larger game fish you may need still longer ones, up to 3 ft. for albacore, school tuna, bonito, etc., and up to 15 ft. for billfish such as sailfish and marlin. And, of course,

Simple knot for joining two lines.

Double thumb knot for tying an end loop on leaders or lines.

Improved clinch knot.

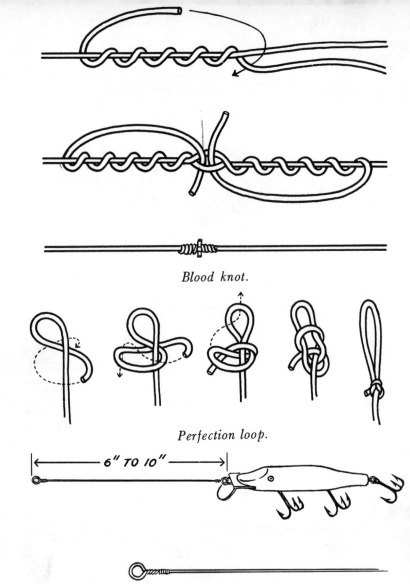

Blood knot.

Perfection loop.

|← 6" TO 10" →|

Permanent wire leader for salt-water lures, showing detail of twisted loop.

Two popular snap swivels.

if you are going after sharks, long leaders of at least 8 or 10 ft. or longer are a must. These fish not only have sharp teeth but their sandpaper hides will quickly cut any line. They also have a habit of spinning and rolling over the line, so that a long leader is an important item in shark fishing.

Two kinds of wire leaders are generally used in salt-water fishing. One is the cable-type leader, usually made of stainless steel. The cable wire comes bare or covered with nylon. In order to make loops for attaching snaps, swivels and hooks to this cable wire it must be crimped with special crimping or swaging pliers. A small brass or copper sleeve or tube is used. The end of the cable leader is passed through the sleeve until it protudes about an inch and a half on the other side. Then the end is doubled back through the sleeve forming a loop. The sleeve is then pinched with the special crimping pliers. The crimping pliers, sleeves and wire are sold by the Berkley Company in a handy leader-crimping kit. They call their cable leader material "Steel-on." These pliers and kits can be bought in many tackle stores.

The other wire material is the single-strand stainless steel, which comes in large coils. Three tools are needed to form eyes and loops with this material: a pair of side-cutting pliers, flat-nose gripping pliers and round-nosed pliers.

The usual procedure in making the eye or loop is to cut off the length of wire you need with cutting pliers. Then grasp the wire about an inch and a half from one end with the round-nosed pliers. If you want a small eye, grab the wire near the extreme ends of the pliers. For larger eyes grab the wire at the lower end of the pliers.

Now, holding the wire tightly between the pliers, twist it around the round nose of the plier until an eye is formed. Then remove the wire from the pliers. Now grasp the eye with gripping pliers and twist the wire where it crosses. This should be done so that the wires interlock. After a few such turns you can make straight turns of the short end of the wire around the main strand. When several such turns have been made and a half-inch or slightly more of wire remains, bend it back sharply toward the eye. Then work it back and forth until it breaks off. This results in a clean break which doesn't protrude to snag or cut.

There are also some special wire-wrapping tools or jigs on the market which can be used to make leaders. But you can make good eyes or loops at home or in the field with the pliers after some practice.

The spin angler will also need different kinds of sinkers and weights, especially if he does still fishing on the bottom in fresh water or salt water. There are many types, such as the round, bank, diamond and pyramid sinkers for salt water and the dipsey sinker for fresh water. It is also a good idea to carry clincher or clamp-on sinkers, to add weight to a line when casting certain lures or baits. For spinning, the type with a rubber core which doesn't damage the line is best.

10

Fresh-water Lures

ALTHOUGH MANY SPECIAL SPINNING LURES have been made since spinning was introduced, almost any lure made for fresh-water or salt-water fishing can be used with a spinning outfit. This includes almost all the bait-casting lures and even some fly-rod lures. When spinning first became popular in fresh water the rods used were all on the light side, and naturally the first lures were also very light. But now, with a wide range of spinning rods, reels and lines to choose from, the spinning angler can use fresh-water lures in all sizes and weights.

The first lures that appeared for spinning were mostly imported from Europe. They took fish, but many of them were poor or mediocre and it wasn't long before they were replaced by American-made lures. Of course, many European lures are still being imported and are being used effectively on our waters.

Many lures have their own "built-in" action. Others must be activated by the angler. Some are designed to work on the surface, others just under the surface and still others down deep near the bottom. Each lure works best under certain conditions, with certain tackle and for specific fish. Their effectiveness also varies with the waters being fished. But in the long run the angler who knows how to use and manipulate the lures so as to bring out

97

their best action catches the most and biggest fish. Often the angler will hit the right combination by luck. Experience will also teach an angler which lure is best under prevailing conditions and waters.

Today the spin angler who fishes streams, ponds, lakes or rivers carries a good assortment of lures to meet varying fishing conditions. Tackle boxes have grown bigger and bigger, to accomodate all these lures.

One of the best all-around lures for fresh-water fishing is the spoon. It comes in many sizes, shapes, weights and materials. The majority are silver in finish, but gold, brass, copper and painted spoons are also made.

The smallest spoons weighing only from $\frac{1}{32}$ to $\frac{1}{4}$ oz. are used with light and ultralight rods for trout, bass and pan fish. The larger spoons, weighing from $\frac{1}{2}$ to 1 oz., are used with the heavier outfits for big trout, Pacific salmon, bass, pike, muskies and lake trout. These may run up to 4 in. or more in length, and are often used for trolling.

Spoons are usually cast and reeled in slowly. They will take fish when reeled or trolled straight but are more appealing when jerked and then allowed to sink and flutter; the process being repeated during the entire retrieve. This imitates a wounded or crippled minnow or small fish. Different depths are tried until the fish are located.

Spinners are similar to spoons in that they depend on flash to attract fish. In addition, they also give off vibrations, which may play an important part in their effectiveness. Like spoons, spinners also come in different sizes, shapes, weights and finishes. The silver finish is the most popular, with gold, copper, brass and painted finishes right behind.

Spinners generally have an oval or elongated leaf-shaped blade which spins on a wire shaft. They may have no extra weights when used for trolling, but for casting they usually have metal heads, lead keels or metal body forms which add weight. There may be one, two or as many as six blades used in tandem on spinners. The multiple-blade spinners are used mostly for trolling.

Spinners come with single, double or treble hooks. Or they may have several single hooks in tandem. The spinners are used alone or have added attractors, such as flies, pork rind, rubber, plastic, bucktail or feather skirts. Still others have plain hooks for use with bait. The well-known June Bug spinner, when used with live bait such as worms or minnows on the trailing hooks, is deadly for black bass, walleyes, pike and big pan fish.

For casting, the weighted-type spinners, such as the French spinners, have become very popular. These are made with short wire shafts on which one or more metal beads or body forms have been added, to provide weight. The blades on these spinners are heavier than those found on other types.

Another type of spinner is the "cherry drifter" or "cherry bobber" which has a balsa-wood body shaped like a teardrop on the wire shaft and a thin spinner blade in front of it. The balsa-wood body is painted red. This lure is used with a small weight on the leader, to get it down close to the bottom. It was originally developed in the Northwest for salmon and steelhead fishing as a substitute for salmon eggs.

The Devon-type lures don't have spinning blades but make use of a body with fins which revolves around a wire shaft. Very small, compact and attractive, they cast well and can be worked deep. To prevent twisted lines, use Devons with a keel weight either on the spinner itself or ahead on the line.

Although the fly rod is best when using tiny dry flies, wet flies, nymphs and streamers, the spin caster can also use these effectively at times. There are plastic floats which provide weight, and a dry fly can be tied on a short leader in front of the float. There are also short weighted lines which can be used to cast flies and other light lures. When fishing for trout a good assortment of local-favorite patterns of dry flies, wet flies and nymphs should be carried. Streamers and bucktails which imitate minnows are also good for trout, bass, pickerel and pan fish. The weighted streamers and bucktails can be cast with the regular spinning lines and rods. These have heavy bodies and can be cast a good distance. They work best when used with the lighter lines and rods.

The bass bugs used with fly rods can be cast with spinning rods with the special short weighted fly-type lines. You can also cast them with the regular mono spinning lines if you add extra weight in the form of lead wire around the body or hook shank. There are also many bass bugs designed for spinning. These are weighted or have plastic bodies heavy enough to cast with regular spinning tackle.

In recent years fresh-water anglers have discovered jigs, which are long time favorites with salt-water anglers. These have heavy metal heads with a single hook, and have feather, bucktail, nylon or rubber skirts. The smaller sizes weigh about $\frac{1}{16}$ or $\frac{1}{8}$ oz. and are ideal for light spinning rods. The heavier ones weighing $\frac{1}{4}$, $\frac{1}{2}$ or 1 oz. are best with the heavier outfits.

Jigs are especially effective for white bass, but will also take trout, black bass, pickerel, walleyes, pike and pan fish. They require a "jerk-and-reel" action in still waters, but in very fast waters they can be drifted with the current, like wet flies or spoons, into deep holes, then retrieved in short, slow jerks.

The wooden, plastic and rubber plug-type lures account for some of the biggest fish in fresh waters. A walk into any well-stocked fishing-tackle store reveals a wide variety of these fish killers. You have a wide choice of sizes, shapes, colors, weights and actions.

Some plugs are made for surface fishing, others dive and still others sink. Surface plugs have cupped heads, big metal lips, propellers or other devices for creating a disturbance, which attracts fish. They usually represent crippled minnows, small fish, frogs, mice and similar creatures. Surface plugs are most effective for shallow- and calm-water fishing.

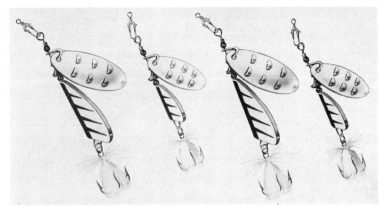

Garcia Abu "Hi-Fi" spinner produces vibrations when reeled. It comes in different finishes and colors.

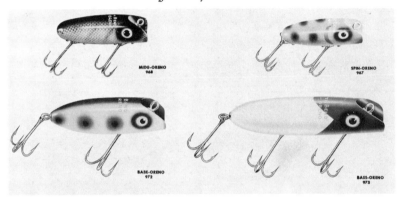

South Bend "Oreno" plug is an old favorite and comes in various sizes and finishes.

Heddin "Spin-I-Diddee" plug weighs $\frac{1}{4}$ oz. and is a surface lure.

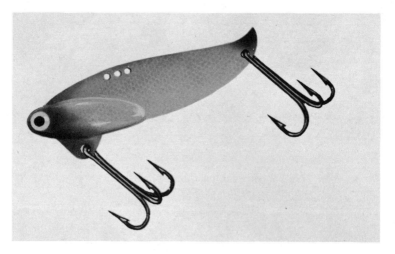

Heddon Sonar is a fast-sinking lure and comes in weights from ¼ to 1 oz.

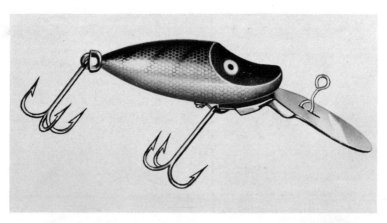

Heddon Deep-dive River Runt Spook travels down deep.

Underwater plugs come in two types—floating and diving types or sinking models. The floating and diving types include those with grooved heads cut at an angle and those with metal lips. They lie on the surface but dive to varying depths when retrieved. These plugs usually have a wobbling, darting or wriggling action. They work best in waters of moderate depths.

Sinking plugs slowly settle to the bottom, and when reeled or jerked slowly hold a certain depth. They are good when fish lie on the bottom in deep water and can be reached only by these sinking plugs and similar weighted lures.

The majority of the plugs made in the past were for bait casting and usually weighed from $\frac{1}{2}$ to $\frac{5}{8}$ oz. They are still good when used with medium or heavy fresh-water spinning rods. The line should test at least 6 lbs. to handle these weights. The larger-sized plugs made for pike, muskies and lake trout or big bass may weigh up to an ounce or more. These are used with the heavier spinning rods and lines testing from 8 to 15 lbs. or more. Most spinning lures now range from $\frac{1}{8}$ to $\frac{1}{2}$ oz. in weight, and plugs in this weight class are most common. However, there are also very light plugs for ultralight spinning which may weigh only $\frac{1}{16}$ oz.

Color isn't too important in a surface plug. Red and white is as good as any color, since the angler can see his plug for quite a distance. But underwater plugs should imitate the colors of the foods found in the waters being fished, or at least they should look something like these foods to the fish. Thus lakes where shiners or other bright silvery minnows or fish are found call for plugs with silver-scale finishes. Where the fish feed on pan fish such as yellow perch or sunfish, plugs with yellow, orange, pink or red bodies are usually best. If the fish in the lake or river you are fishing feed on drab-colored darters, stone catfish or small bullheads, use brown or black plugs. If frogs are eaten by the fish plugs with white or pale-yellow bellies and green backs are the ones to use.

Plugs are good for daytime or night fishing. The fish are attracted by the "plopping" or "gurgling" noise and commotion on the water that most plugs produce when reeled in at a slow or moderate speed. Surface plugs that pop or create a fuss are best when fished very slow. Most crippled minnows, frogs or mice do not swim without rests. They travel a few inches or feet, then stop, then move again, then stop, etc. Try to imitate this action with your surface plug. About the only exception is when schools of fish are chasing minnows on the surface. Then a fast moving surface plug such as a torpedo type will often take them.

Underwater plugs should be given a jerk at regular intervals to increase their effectiveness. Sometimes stopping the plug a second or two and then resuming the retrieve does the trick.

Sinking plugs should be allowed to settle almost to the bottom. Then just twitch the rod tip and reel in a few inches of line, twitch again and reel. The idea is to give the big, lazy bass or other fish plenty of time to see the lure and to tease him into striking it. These fish resting on the bottom are not feeding, but the proper lure with the right teasing action will often bring a strike. Sharp hooks are a must for sinking plugs.

In fact, all plugs or other lures should be examined carefully to see that the hooks are needle-sharp. Many fish are lost or fail to get hooked because of dull hooks. This is especially important when using ultralight and other light spinning tackle with sensitive tips and light lines.

Then we have the many natural, lifelike imitations of natural baits which are made of soft rubber or plastic materials. Such lures have become very popular in recent years and have taken many big fish, especially bass. There are rubber or plastic imitations of various insects, such as hellgrammites, nymphs, grasshoppers, crickets, beetles and spiders. Some of these are un-weighted and must be cast with the lightest spinning tackle or have a small clincher sinker added up ahead on the leader.

There are also rubber or plastic imitations of such baits as

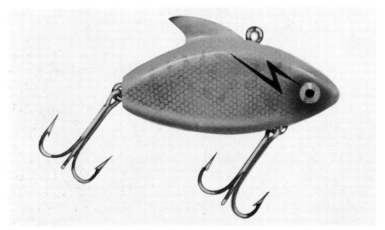

Heddon "Super-Sonic" attracts fish both by sight and sound.

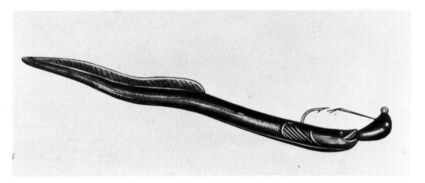

Creme Lure black plastic eel has weighted jig head and weed-less hook.

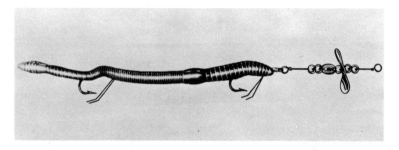

Creme Lure plastic worm has small spinner and weedless hooks.

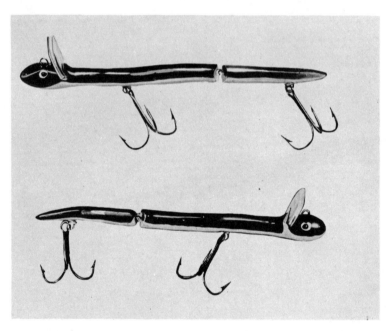

Garcia's Eelet is an imitation of a small fresh-water eel and comes in weights from $\frac{3}{16}$ to $\frac{9}{16}$ oz.

crayfish, frogs, salamanders, eels and minnows. The minnows usually have a lip or plate to give them a built-in action and can often be reeled in straight. But most of the other lures of this type must be jerked or twitched, to give them action.

One very popular lure at present is the plastic or rubber worm. These are now available in various lengths, weights and colors. There are natural-colored worms resembling night crawlers, but others come in black, white, yellow, cream, red, green, blue-spotted and in combinations of these colors.

The worms are sold plain in plastic bags of varying numbers. These can be hooked with a single hook, but you can also buy plastic worms with two or three hooks already attached. Still other baits of this type come with spinners in front or metal jig heads, to provide weight for casting and rapid sinking. Some of the worms also have silver or gold metal bands. Most of the plastic worms are fished slowly on the bottom, being bounced or twitched or dragged along very slowly.

Every fresh-water spin angler should carry two or three jars of pork rind in different sizes. Pork rind can be used alone or with another lure to catch pan fish, black bass, pickerel, pike, muskies and many other fresh-water fish. Strips of pork rind used alone are worked, like streamer flies, in short jerks or long sweeps of the rod tip. When skittered along on top of the water they are deadly for pickerel. Their white color and attractive flutter makes them appealing. When used alone the pork rind strips can be fairly long and wide. You may need a few split shot or a small clincher sinker on the leader to cast them out. Shorter and narrower strips can be used on the tail hooks of plugs, spoons or spinners.

Pork chunks can be cut into various sizes and shapes, but the most popular is the shape of a frog. The legs consist of the rind or short pieces of wool flannel inserted into the body. The front part of the chunk is thick, with the fat left on. These can be used in the natural white pork color, but many anglers like to dye them green or yellow. Pork chunks are best when used with a single weedless hook and fished on top of lily pads, in weed beds and grasses where frogs are found.

You can cut your own pork rind strips or chunks, but most tackle stores carry them in jars, prepared and ready for use. It's a good idea to always carry pork rind or chunks on every fishing trip.

There is also another pork lure, the "black eel," which is a tapering, narrow strip of pork dyed black and hooked with a single hook. It may be anywhere from 5 to 10 in. long. They come already prepared in jars, and can be used with one or two hooks. They are used, like the plastic worms, on or near the bottom, and are reeled, twitched and jerked as slowly as possible.

11

Salt-water Lures

Many of the fresh-water lures described and illustrated in the previous chapter can also be used in salt-water fishing, especially with the lighter spinning rods and lines. However, salt-water lures are usually somewhat heavier, the hooks are stronger and they can take more wear and tear. This is only natural, since salt-water corrosion and the larger fish are tough on lures. Lures made especially for salt water are usually the most dependable and best for spinning in the ocean.

An old-time lure used by surf casters is the metal squid. These lures are still effective when used with spinning outfits. Metal squids come in dozens of different sizes, shapes and weights. Most of them imitate some short, broad fish, such as mullet, anchovy, menhaden or herring. However, a few are narrow and long, and simulate bait fish such as sand eels, spearing or silversides, and salt-water minnows of various kinds.

Metal squids are made from lead, block tin or other metals. Block-tin squids are shiny and bright; the other metals have to be chrome-plated, since they are dull and tarnish quickly. Usually one hook is used in metal squids, and this may be embedded in the squid or attached so that it swings. The plain squid will often catch fish, but most anglers add a strip of pork rind or tie white, yellow or red feathers or hair around the hook.

Metal squids will run in weight from $\frac{1}{4}$ oz. up to 3 or 4 oz. For surf spinning metal squids from $\frac{3}{4}$ oz. up to 3 oz. are the sizes usually used, depending on the rod and line. Although primarily a casting lure used from shore or boats, metal squids can also be trolled to take a wide variety of salt-water species. Each squid has a different action and depth at which it works; some come in fairly straight, while others work rapidly from side to side. Reeling at a moderate speed will bring out the best action. Sometimes fast reeling will produce more strikes; at other times slow reeling is best.

In recent years many anglers have started using another lure more or less as a substitute for metal squids. This is the popular Hopkins "No-Eql" lure, which is flat and rippled with multi-mirrored indentations along its sides, which glitter and shine. It is made of solid stainless steel and comes in various sizes for casting from surf or boats and also for trolling. It will catch such fish as striped bass, bluefish, channel bass, pollock, barracuda, bonito and dolphin.

Spoons can be used to good effect by the spin fisherman in many types of salt-water angling. They come in the same finishes and shapes as the fresh-water spoons described earlier. However, they are generally heavier, thicker and have stronger hooks. Usually the treble hook is replaced by a heavy salt-water single hook. The most popular finish on salt-water spoons is chrome. Some are nickel-plated or gold-plated for salt-water use. Still others are painted in various colors. And many spoons have bucktail wound around the hook. White, yellow or red-and-white bucktail is generally used.

For spin fishing in bays, inlets, rivers and on flats the smaller spoons up to 3 or 4 in. are best. They usually run up to an ounce in weight. The larger sizes are used for trolling. Spoons offer

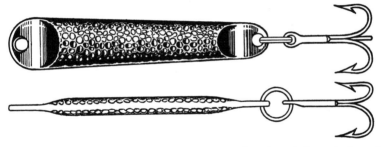

Hopkins "No-Eql" metal lures are made of stainless steel and are used in jigging, casting or trolling from shore and boats.

Barracuda nylon jig comes in different weights and colors for many salt-water fishes.

Tony Accetta Jigaroo is available in weights from $\frac{1}{8}$ to $3\frac{1}{2}$ ozs. It's a jig with spinner combination.

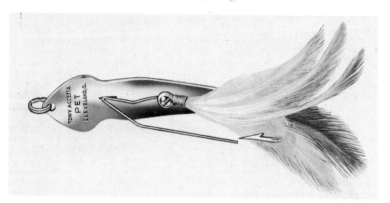

Tony Accetta Pet spoon is widely used for spin casting in salt water from shore or boat.

Creek Chub Surfster surface plug is available in $\frac{3}{4}$, $1\frac{7}{8}$ and $2\frac{1}{2}$ oz. weights.

quite a bit of wind resistance and you can't cast them as far as some lures if they are made of thin metal. There are some heavier-gauge spoons, which are also more compact, and these will sail out pretty far. But spoons are good fish takers and a small assortment in various sizes should be carried by the spin angler.

When using spoons, slow reeling or trolling usually produces the best results. An erratic retrieve works on many occasions. Here you jerk the rod tip, then pause, let the spoon sink and flutter, then speed up or jerk again, repeating this procedure during the entire retrieve. This imitates a crippled bait fish and often brings a smashing strike.

Spinners also take their share of salt-water fish. They, too, depend on flash and motion to attract fish. In this respect they are similar to spoons. The revolving blade may also give off vibrations which attract fish. But spinners are difficult to cast any distance and are used mainly in trolling. Nickel-plated, chrome or stainless steel spinners are preferred for salt-water use.

Although spinners will catch fish when used alone, they are usually used in conjunction with feathers, pork rind or natural baits such as seaworms or small bait fish. A strip of squid or fillet of fish will also work at times. Two popular types of spinners are the June Bug and Cape Cod spinners. Spinners should be trolled very slowly at varying depths until the fish are located. They can also be let out in the current from a bridge, pier or boat and "worked" slowly back against the current. For bottom fish, such as summer flounders or fluke, they are drifted deep with a sinker. In a strong tide a trolling weight or keel is sometimes needed ahead of the spinner, to keep it down.

When it comes to plugs, we find that there are almost as many varieties and types used in salt water as in fresh. Here again the plugs made especially for salt-water use are larger, heavier and stronger. The hooks, especially, should be of strong, heavy wire.

Weak hooks are quickly straightened by big fish, even when light spinning lures are used. There are still many wooden plugs on the market, but more and more plastic types are replacing the wooden plugs. They are more durable and have permanent colors.

Since most bait fish found in salt water are colored with blue or green backs and silver or white sides and bellies, these colors are often effective in a plug. All yellow, red and white or silver plugs are also good. For light spinning, salt-water plugs from $\frac{1}{2}$ to 1 oz. in weight are used, while for casting with heavier tackle and for surf fishing, plugs running up to 3 oz. may be used.

Every spin angler should carry an assortment of plugs in both surface and underwater models. The surface popping and torpedo shapes are deadly for most game fish that chase bait fish on top. Underwater plugs are needed when fish are down deep. Some plugs have a built-in action, and just plain reeling will often catch fish. Others, like the poppers or torpedo shapes, must be jerked at regular intervals to create a splash or wake. Try to imitate a frantic bait fish seeking to escape from larger fish, and you'll catch fish on such plugs. For best results buy your plugs from a tackle store near the location where you plan to fish. Then you won't go wrong as to size, weight, color or action.

The most versatile lure a spin angler can use in salt waters is the jig. Also known as bucktails, bugeyes, bullheads and barracudas, these lures are made to order for spinning tackle. They are compact and can be cast like a bullet on light lines. Best of all, they appeal to most fish, often catching bottom species as well as game fish. They are especially effective in the warmer waters of Florida, the Bahamas, Bermuda, the Caribbean and Mexico. Even in northern waters they often take fish when other lures fail to produce.

Jigs come in different weights, colors, sizes and dressings. Most of them are similar in that they have a heavy lead or other metal

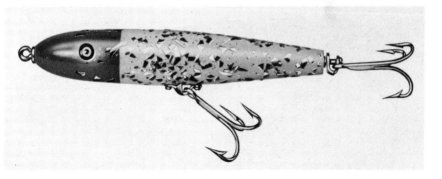

Pflueger Ballerina plug is a surface lure used for many salt-water game fish.

Pflueger Lastword spoon is made for casting in salt water from surf and boats.

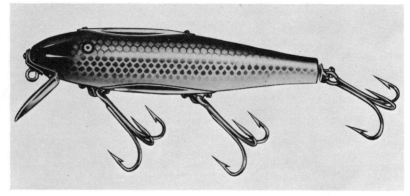

Pflueger Mustang is 5 in. long and weighs $1\frac{1}{2}$ oz.

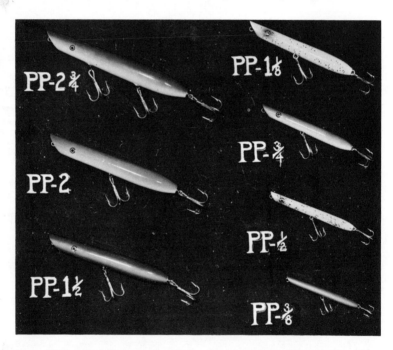

Stan Gibbs Pencil Popper plugs come in the different sizes and weights shown. They are surface lures and attract stripers, blues, weakfish, snook, tarpon and many other salt-water species.

head, with feathers, bucktail or other hair, nylon or rubber or plastic skirts wrapped around the hook. The metal head is usually chromed or painted in various colors. Those with white, yellow or red heads predominate in salt-water fishing.

Most of the jigs range in weight from $\frac{1}{8}$ oz. to 3 or 4 oz. The single hooks molded into the head run from size 1/0 up to 8/0, depending on the size and weight of the jig. There are heavier and longer jigs, which are used in big-game fishing with conventional tackle. For spinning and light trolling the smaller sizes work best.

Jigs are used both in casting and trolling from shore and boats. They are trolled fast for such speedsters as small tuna, albacore, bonito and mackerel. For other fish a moderate or slow speed is better. Jerk the rod at regular intervals while trolling.

When fishing from the surf, small boats, bridges and piers, jigs can be adapted to conditions and to the water being fished. When fish are feeding on the surface, chasing bait fish, the jig is cast out and immediately reeled in fairly fast or at a moderate speed. On other occasions they can be cast out, allowed to sink a few feet, then jerked, allowed to sink, jerked, etc. They can also be cast out and then slowly bounced along the bottom all the way in. At other times you can lower the jig to the bottom and work it up and down so that it dances about, just off the bottom. This can be done from an anchored or drifting boat. In a current, jigs can often be cast across and slightly up, then allowed to drift down and sink as they are carried downstream. Jigs are excellent lures in fast currents and deep water, since they sink quickly and offer less resistance to the water than other lures. In combination with light spinning lines they enable an angler to fish depths seldom reached before.

A good assortment of jigs in various sizes and colors are a must for the salt-water spin angler. They take up little room, and a dozen or two can be carried in a small tackle box or bag. You need plenty, too, because jigs often get hung up on the bottom and are lost.

Another lure called the "jig" is actually more like a metal squid or spoon. However, it is usually jigged up and down, like the jigs, under the boat. This is the diamond jig, which has four flat sides and a treble hook attached to the tail. Some have a single hook molded into the body. These small diamond jigs, often called weakfish or mackerel jigs, are used for those fish. But the most common type of diamond jig has a treble hook and bright finish of chrome or nickel. Diamond jigs come in various sizes and weights from 1 to 10 oz. They can be cast and reeled and trolled to take fish. But the most popular way to fish them is to let them down until they hit bottom and then alternately jerk them up quickly and let them settle again. This "jigging" will catch almost anything that swims in the ocean. The fish will usually be hooked in the mouth, but sometimes the hooks will grab some other part of the body.

Other lures used in salt water in various areas are the eelskin lures and rigged eels popular on the East Coast for striped bass and bluefish. These will also work at times in southern waters for cobia, snook and other species.

Rubber-tube lures and rubber imitations of various fish foods, such as small bait fish, squid, eels, seaworms and shrimp, are also being made. Usually soft and flexible, most of these imitations have no built-in action and must be manipulated and worked with the rod tip after being cast or while being trolled.

Salt-water spinning anglers also make use of pork rind in various sizes and lengths. These are added to spinners, spoons or plugs, or used on separate connection alone. Larger and longer strips of pork rind, up to 10 or 12 in. in length, are being used in offshore trolling for big-game fish.

When using any salt-water lure a certain amount of care is required to prevent rust and corrosion. If possible, try to wash the lure in fresh water and let it dry before putting it back into the tackle box. When you come home open up the tackle box and let the lures dry out. If you apply a thin coat of oil on the metal parts and hooks, they will not rust as readily. If the hooks do rust badly, remove them and replace them with new ones. If this cannot be done, discard the lure or use it for small fish only. Many a big fish in salt water is lost when a rusty hook breaks off or straightens out.

12

Spinning Accessories

BESIDES THE RODS, reels, lines and lures, the spin fisherman needs many accessories to make his fishing safer and more comfortable and productive. Some of these fall into the class of "gadgets" and are not absolutely necessary. But others are essential and may play a big part in your fishing success.

Take boots, waders and clothes, for example. There are some spots which you can fish without boots or waders, but other spots demand that you wade out into the stream, river or surf to reach the fish or the most productive areas. Or take clothes. If you are comfortably dressed and have the proper waterproof jackets, parkas and pants, you can fish in rainy or stormy weather when other anglers without this foul-weather gear have to give up and pack in. This often means that you have good fishing that other anglers miss.

Here are the more important accessories which a spin angler can use in fresh- and salt-water fishing. First are boots. These are a must for any spin angler who fishes a trout stream, river, marshy lake shore or the surf. There are many kinds of boots on the market, but be sure to get the special light type made for fishermen. Heavy work boots should be avoided. Boots will serve the purpose when fishing shallow streams, rivers or surf where you

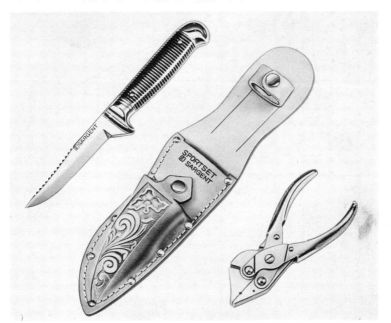

No spin angler is completely equipped without a good knife and pliers. This set can be carried in the leather sheath.

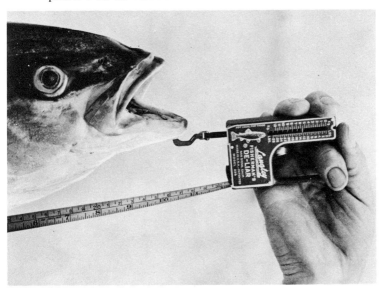

A pocket-size scale for weighing that big one is handy to have. There are sizes for both fresh- and salt-water fish.

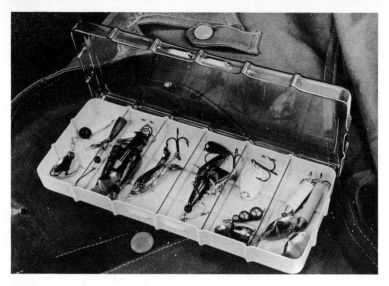

Bill DeWitt plastic lure box is popular for holding small and medium-size fishing lures.

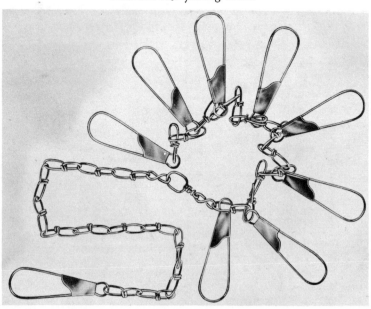

This fish stringer with individual clips is popular with fresh-water fishermen.

don't have to wade out too far. Hip boots are best for this purpose. If you fish from a boat in salt water or on a large lake
where spray from the waves come into the boat, you can use
short boots which come up to the ankles or knees. These short
boots are also good for fishing in rainy weather. You can wear
waterproof pants over them to keep out the water.

For deep wading in streams, rivers, lakes or ocean surf, waist-
high waders are used. Waders come in various materials, such as
plastic, rubberized canvas and all-rubber. Plastic waders are light
and excellent for hot weather or when walking long distances.
They don't stand up as well around rocks as other types, and
therefore aren't as popular for salt-water fishing along rocky
shores. But for light stream fishing they are fine and can be
carried in a small space when rolled up.

The heavier rubberized-canvas or all-rubber waders are strong
and will serve for most cold-water fishing in fresh and salt waters
encountered early in the spring, fall and winter or in stormy,
rainy weather. You can wear heavy underwear, shirts, pants and
woolen socks in them, and fish in fair comfort under such conditions. These waders are not too comfortable for walking long
distances, especially in hot weather. But they are rugged and
stand up well from wear and tear.

Waders come mainly in two types — those with stocking feet
and those with boot feet. The stocking-foot waders require some
kind of wading shoes in addition. The boot-foot waders are permanently attached to the rest of the waders. Boot-foot waders
take less time to put on and are preferred for salt-water and
big-water fishing. The stocking-foot waders are best for small
trout streams and fresh water, especially where you have to do a
lot of walking.

Most waders come with rubber heels and soles, and for fishing
from sandy beaches, gravel and pebble bottoms or for wading
quiet waters they serve the purpose. But when used in deep, fast
rivers and along slippery rocks, waders with felt soles are better

and safer. If these are not attached permanently to the soles of your waders you can buy a pair of wading sandals and felt or hob-nail soles. There are also many types of ice creepers and chains which can be worn over waders or boots to assume a grip on slippery rocks and jetties.

A jacket of some kind is also needed by the spin angler for salt- or fresh-water fishing. When fishing from a boat an ordinary jacket will often serve the purpose. For salt-water use, a water-proof jacket is better because of the spray, mist and dampness. When the spray is heavy and in rainy weather a waterproof parka jacket and pants are needed. These are also worn by most surf anglers, together with boots or waders.

For the spin angler fishing a trout stream, river or lake, a jacket with plenty of pockets is worn. There are many types on the market that have pockets of all sizes to accommodate all the lures and gadgets which are carried.

A hat of some kind is needed to protect the hair, head and eyes from rain, spray and sun. You can, of course, use any old hat for this purpose, but there are special fishing hats which are light and water-repellent. For salt water use, a cap with a long peak or visor is best.

Spin anglers also need containers or pouches for their lures. For the fisherman wading fresh-water streams or rivers, the small transparent tackle boxes which can be slipped into a pocket are very handy. These have separate compartments for holding the lures. There are larger sizes, which can be used by boat fishermen. Stream or shore fishermen can also get one of the special apron-style fishing vests, which have large pockets for lures and acces-sories.

If you fish from a boat, pier or shore you can get one of the shoulder bags for carrying lures, reels, lines, sinkers and even a lunch or thermos bottle. The larger ones are best for salt-water fishing, while the smaller ones are used by fresh-water anglers. Small shoulder bags are also worn by some surf fishermen. But

Gaffs are used when boating big fish. There are various sizes, lengths and strengths on the market.

Spin anglers often find handy the kind of vests usually used by fly fishermen, for holding lures and other items.

This combination insect repellent and sun-tan application is handy for the angler who stays outdoors for long periods.

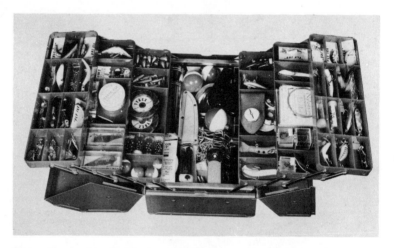

Nowadays a big tackle box is almost a must for the spin angler. To hold all the different-sized lures, floats, hooks, sinkers, knife, stringer and other items, it must have plenty of trays.

here many prefer a belt, around which they can attach or string small pouches or lure containers. This leaves their hands free for casting, carrying and using the rod and for hauling fish.

The boat angler in fresh or salt water who takes along a lot of lures and tackle will find some kind of tackle-box ideal. They come in various sizes and materials, such as steel, aluminium, fiberglass and wood. Most of these are good for fresh water, but for salt-water use get one of the boxes made from plastic, fiberglass or wood. And you need a pretty big one for salt water, to hold the larger reels, lures and other equipment.

For landing or boating a fish, a landing net or gaff is required. The angler fishing a small stream for trout and bass can use one of the smaller nets, which are worn on the person. For landing big fish you need a larger landing net or gaff. And for surf fishing from the beach, rocky shores and jetties you need suitable gaffs. The beach or wading fisherman can use a short gaff, which is worn on a belt. But for gaffing a fish from high rocks or a jetty you need a gaff with a long handle. Boat anglers also need gaffs with longer handles for big fish. Small salt-water fish can be boated with landing nets.

After you land or boat your fish you have to keep them alive or preserved. Fish stringers and creels of various kinds are on the market for this purpose. The wading fisherman who fishes a small stream for trout or bass will find a willow creel handy. If this is too bulky, you can always get a lighter creel, made of matting, canvas or plastic.

The shore fisherman will find a cotton cord or chain fish stringer useful. A fish bag can also be used; an ordinary potato sack will often serve the purpose or you can buy a regular net-type fish bag. The boat angler can also use such stringers if his boat doesn't have a built-in fish well. The stringers made from chain, with safety pin snaps, are quick and easy to use. Surf anglers like long fish stringers made of venetian blind cord, nylon anchor line or clothes line.

The salt-water boat fisherman will find a large fish box more useful for his purpose. Of course, some of the larger boats have built-in fish boxes, and ice can be carried to keep the catch fresh. If there is no built-in fish box on the boat you can use one of the plastic garbage cans as a fish box or bait container. These come in different sizes and have tight-fitting covers.

Don't forget a good pair of pliers. In fact, if you haven't a pair of combination pliers it's a good idea to carry one pair each of cutting and gripping pliers. A pair of long-nosed pliers are useful in removing hooks from a fish's mouth. A special hook disgorger can also be carried for this purpose. Cutting pliers should be strong enough to cut through a large salt-water hook. To be prepared for emergencies a tool kit should be carried. This can have (besides the pliers) a file, small hammer, small saw that cuts wood and metal, some screwdrivers and any tools you think you may need. Of course, you can't carry this around with you, but it can be taken aboard a boat or at least kept in the car. A first-aid kit should also be taken along.

An oil can, reel grease and small sharpening stones are needed for lubricating reels and sharpening hooks and knives.

To protect your face and hands from the sun, a sun-tan lotion is helpful, especially for salt-water fishing. Sun glasses also help to protect the eyes and Polaroid types help in locating fish below the surface of the water. For locating fish breaking on top of the water or for spotting diving gulls which may pinpoint a school of fish, a good pair of binoculars is useful.

During the summer months and in tropical climes an insect repellent is something you need if you want to fish in peace, especially at night or dusk.

To weigh that big one you need a scale. Some fishermen's scales also have a tape ruler for measuring fish.

For night fishing or for finding your way back at night in the woods or on the water you need a searchlight or headlight. The latter is preferred by most boat fishermen and surf anglers, since it can be worn around the head or neck and leaves your hands free for fishing or running a boat.

Finally, we have such items as refrigerator boxes, picnic bags, thermos bottles or jugs, drinking cups, etc., which are great for carrying food and drinks.

13

Natural Baits

SPINNING TACKLE has been hailed by most fresh- and salt-water anglers as tops for casting light artificial lures. Less publicized but equally important is the fact that spin tackle is also ideal for using natural baits. Both fresh- and salt-water spin fishermen have discovered that they can use the live baits more effectively with their outfits than the anglers with conventional tackle.

One big reason for this is that you can cast the soft, light natural baits farther without snapping off and losing the bait. With many baits, such as large worms, minnows or bait fish, crayfish, frogs, crabs, etc., you can cast a surprising distance without any additional weight. And even with the lightest baits all you need is a small sinker or a tiny float or bobber in order to cast way out.

Because of the light lines used in spinning you can allow a bait to swim or drift more naturally. The almost invisible line makes it look like the bait is not attached. You can also use small, fine-wire hooks, because there is less strain placed on a hook by the flexible spin rods and thin lines. And if you do have to use a sinker for bottom fishing or trolling, you can use a much lighter one than with the heavier lines used on conventional tackle. It all adds up to more fish, bigger fish and more sport and fun.

Fresh-water Baits—Earthworms easily rank number one on the fresh-water angler's bait list. They can be bought, dug or raised in wooden boxes. Worms like rich, moist soil such as is found in gardens. Here you'll find the smaller angleworms or garden worms. The big, red night crawlers like lawns, golf courses and other grassy places, where they emerge after dark and can be caught with a dim flashlight. Just grab them near the hole, then pull steadily. They are most plentiful after rain.

Keep worms in a container of damp soil or wet moss, in a cool spot out of the sun. For keeping worms over extended periods large boxes or containers are best. For a day or two a small container, such as an ordinary bait bucket, will serve.

When still fishing a small worm can be hooked through the center. For drifting, casting or trolling, hook a worm once through the head. Some fish, such as black bass, catfish and suckers, like two, three or more worms on a hook. Earthworms are used mainly for trout, bass and pan fish, but will catch most fresh-water fish.

The water insects found in streams, lakes and rivers are readily eaten by many fish and make good baits. One of the best known is the hellgrammite, which is used mainly in rivers for small-mouth bass. Known by many names all over the country, the hellgrammite looks like a fat, black centipede with two pincers on the head. They can give you a good bite, so grab them behind the head.

Hellgrammites are sometimes sold in tackle stores or by bait dealers, but can also be obtained in fast, shallow rapids or riffles of streams and rivers. An old window screen can be held in the water and the rocks upstream from it turned over. The current will sweep the hellgrammites on to the screen. They can be kept for days in damp grass or moss.

The best way to hook a hellgrammite is under the broad collar. You can drift a hellgrammite with the current or let it sink in a quiet pool. But keep them off the bottom, since they crawl under rocks. Besides small-mouth bass, hellgrammites will also catch big trout, walleyes and large pan fish.

Various kinds of nymphs, such as the dragonfly nymph, Mayfly nymph and stonefly nymph, also make fine baits for trout, bass, pan fish and other fish. They live in the mud, silt or under rocks in brooks, streams and lakes. You can obtain them by digging and probing in the mud, turning over the rocks and by drawing small nets or seines through the weeds. For hooking these delicate water insects use a tiny, fine-wire hook. For best results, fish them by drifting them in a current or jerking them slowly through the water.

The caddis worm or larva is another good water insect for trout and pan fish. They are found clinging to the rocks of streams and lakes or crawling on the bottom. Caddis worms are small white or cream-colored worms which build cases around themselves from bits of sand, tiny stones, sticks or leaves. You have to break open the case to get the worm out. Hook them through the head with a tiny hook. Sometimes two or three caddis worms on a hook work better than one.

When it comes to land insects, the grasshopper is one of the choice baits to use. They are found in fields and gardens, where they can be caught by hand or with a small butterfly net. Keep them in a small wooden box or can, with some leaves or grass.

Crickets are also found in many of the same places as grasshoppers. However, they remain more hidden under stones, hay, straw or leaves. Some anglers also raise crickets in large tubs. They can also be bought from bait dealers in some sections of the country.

When hooking grasshoppers or crickets use a small, fine-wire hook and run it under the collar, avoiding the head. For best results, use them alive on the surface, so that they kick around and make a commotion. It won't be long before a trout, bass or big pan fish comes up and takes it. To cast these baits with a

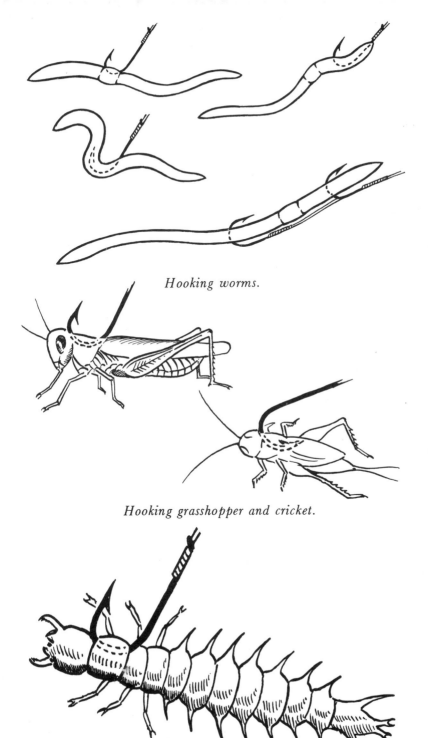

Hooking worms.

Hooking grasshopper and cricket.

Hooking hellgrammite.

Hooking minnows.

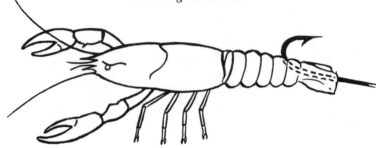

Hooking crayfish.

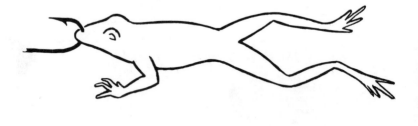

Hooking a frog.

spin rod you can use a plastic float. They can also be fished under the water with a split-shot sinker or two.

The many kinds of minnows found in streams, rivers and lakes are great baits for most game fish. The most popular are the chubs, shiners, dace, blunt-nose and fat-head minnows. Minnows are now raised commercially in many areas, and can be bought in most tackle stores and from bait dealers and boat stations in season. If you want to catch your own you will need an umbrella net or seine. Before buying such a seine, however, check your local and state laws for regulations governing minnow seining.

Minnows are kept alive in bait cages or tanks for long periods. During a fishing trip a minnow bucket is needed. There are several ways you can hook a minnow. The most popular for still fishing is through the back. For trolling or casting, hook them through both lips. Dead minnows are trolled behind spinners or drifted in the current. In such cases they are "sewed" on the hook, to form a bend which causes them to spin. There are also special minnow harnesses which can be used.

Other small fish which can be used for bait include small catfish, suckers, darters, sunfish and yellow perch.

The crayfish is another excellent bait for small-mouth bass, and will also catch carp, catfish and large pan fish. They look like small lobsters but rarely grow to more than a few inches. Living in streams, rivers and lakes in weeds, under stones in burrows, they can be caught at night in traps baited with dead fish or meat or by hand with a flashlight and small net. In the daytime, turn over the stones or poke in the weeds.

The best crayfish for bait are the soft-shelled ones that have cast off their hard coverings. But the smaller hard-shelled ones will also catch fish. A crayfish tail, peeled to expose the meat, is also a good bait, especially for pan fish.

Hook a hard crayfish through the tail, running the hook up from the bottom. A soft one must be tied to the hook with fine thread or with rubber bands.

The smaller leopard frog, pickerel frog, green frog and young bull frog will often fool a big bass, trout, pickerel, pike or muskie. You can catch frogs in shallow water or along the shore, by hand or with a net. Keep them in wet grass or leaves in a container. Hook them through both lips or the leg. Cast the frog out and let it swim around on the surface. Keep it moving. When a fish grabs the frog let him swim with it, feeding slack line. Then the fish will usually stop to swallow the frog. When he starts moving off again let the line tighten and set the hook.

Salmon eggs are used by steelhead fishermen, especially during the winter months. The large eggs can be used singly or with several on a hook. Clusters of a dozen or more eggs are also used, and these must be held with the leader loop or tied around the hook with fine thread. Clusters of salmon eggs are also wrapped in tiny bags or maline cloth or other fine netting. These "strawberries" can be tied up in advance and then impaled on the hook, or the eggs and netting can be tied around the hook. The point and barb of the hook should protrude to facilitate hooking.

Salmon eggs can be bought in most tackle stores, already packed in jars singly or in clusters or strawberries. The fresh eggs taken from a recently killed female salmon or steelhead trout are preferred by most veteran anglers.

This covers the main fresh-water baits, but there are many others, such as salamanders, fresh-water clams and mussels, snails, toads, mice and various doughball and stink baits which can be used.

Salt-water Baits—The salt-water spin fisherman is using more and more artificial lures, but natural baits still predominate in this fishing. It pays to find out which baits have been producing in your local area recently and take such baits along when you go fishing. Most experienced salt-water fishermen carry several kinds of bait to increase their chances of catching fish.

Seaworms are consistent producers of salt-water fish and are especially favored along the North Atlantic coast. The clam

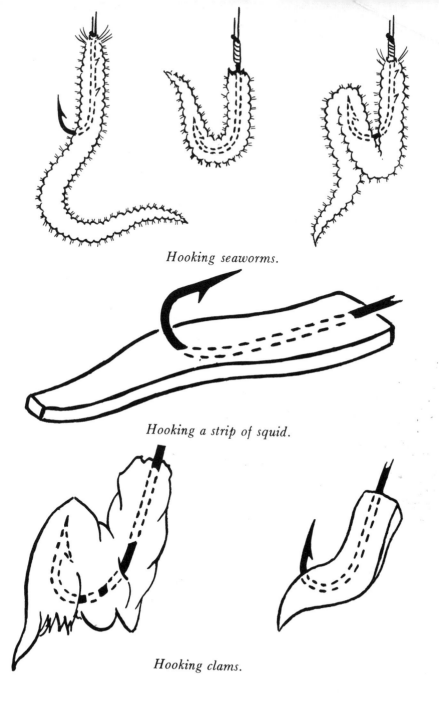

Hooking seaworms.

Hooking a strip of squid.

Hooking clams.

BIG CLAWS REMOVED

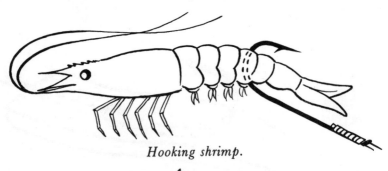

Hooking crabs.

Hooking shrimp.

Hooking dead bait fish

worm, also called the sand worm, is widely used. This worm has a bluish or greenish irridescent back, pink or red undersides, and many legs. The clam worm of the Atlantic is similar to the pile worms or rock worms of the Pacific coast.

Another popular worm on the East Coast is the bloodworm, a pink, smooth worm which shoots out a long proboscis with four tiny black jaws when disturbed. Similar species are found on the Pacific coast, but they aren't numerous there.

Seaworms can be dug with a garden fork on tidal mud and sand flats. They are also found among mussels, under rocks and in seaweed. Seaworms can be bought in many coastal tackle stores.

For big fish, one or two whole worms can be hooked behind the head and draped on a hook. A whole worm can also be used behind spinners, for trolling. For smaller fish a short piece of worm can be used. Seaworms will take striped bass, weakfish, tautog or blackfish, flounders, sea bass and porgies in the Atlantic, and corbina, spotfin and yellowfin croakers and surf perch in the Pacific.

Clams of various kinds make top baits for ocean fishing. There are many kinds, such as the big surf clams, hard-shell clams, soft-shell clams, razor and jackknife clams. They can often be found washed up on the beaches after storms or can be dug in the mud and sand. Clams are also sold by bait dealers and tackle stores in areas where they are plentiful. Whole clams are used for the larger fish, such as cod and striped bass. Smaller pieces are used for such fish as porgies, flounders, corbina, croakers and surf perch.

The mussels found in most salt waters can also be used for bait. They can be picked by the bushel off rocks, piles or mussel beds at low tide. They are soft and should be wrapped around the hook with fine thread. Mussels can be used for flounders, blackfish or tautog, porgies, corbina, kelp bass, croakers and surf perch.

Other shellfish, such as oysters, scallops, snails, whelks and conchs, can also be used for bait.

When it comes to a good versatile bait it's hard to find a better one than squid. This is the jet-propelled cousin of the octopus found and used along both the Pacific and Atlantic coasts. Squid are occasionally found stranded on our beaches, or are caught with dip nets or snagged with treble hooks when they come close to piers or shore. However, the most dependable source is the local bait dealer or tackle store. They can also be bought in many fish markets. Both fresh and frozen squid can be used for bait.

Whole squid are rigged for trolling for swordfish, marlin and tuna. A whole squid can also be fished on the bottom for striped bass, channel bass and other large fish. However, most squid are cut into strips of varying sizes. These strips can also be added to the hooks of plugs, spinners, spoons and other lures. Small pieces of squid can be used for most ocean-bottom fish.

Crabs of many kinds make good baits. They are found in the surf, ocean, bays, inlets and salt and brackish rivers. Crabs are caught in wire cages, traps and scoop nets. Hard crabs, such as small green crabs, fiddler crabs and blue crabs, are used whole, with the hook piercing the shell from bottom to top. Larger hard crabs can be cut into sections. But soft-shelled or shedder crabs make the best bait. Blue crabs in the soft stage can often be bought in fish markets or from bait dealers. The other crabs have to be caught with nets or traps along the beaches or bays.

Soft-shell or shedder crabs are tender, and must be tied to the hook with fine thread. Rubber bands can also be used to hold the bait. Crabs must be kept on ice or in salt water until used. Many ocean fish will take a crab bait.

Somewhat similar as a bait are the lobsters, especially the spiny lobsters or salt-water crayfish found in warmer waters. These are caught in traps or by hand, and only the soft meat in the tail is used. They will catch such fish as bonefish, snappers, groupers, grunts and many other fish found in the same waters as the lobsters.

Shrimps and prawns are also widely used for bait, especially in Florida and the Gulf of Mexico. However, northern anglers along the Atlantic Coast also use shrimp, both the large jumbo varieties sold in fish markets and the smaller grass shrimp. Grass shrimp are widely used in bays for chumming for weakfish and striped bass. They draw the fish to the boat, where a small shrimp or other bait on a hook will catch them. A spinning outfit is ideal for such fishing, since the small shrimp can be drifted in the current naturally.

Larger live shrimps are sold mostly in southern waters by bait dealers and boat liveries. Anglers can often catch their own at night by using lanterns and scoop nets. Shrimp are hooked through the tail or back, for best results. Dead or frozen shrimp can also be used, but live shrimp are preferred. They'll take such fish as snook, redfish (channel bass), sea trout, bonefish, pompano, sheepshead, snappers, groupers, grunts and a multitude of other game and bottom fish.

Sand bugs or sand crabs, which are found burrowing in the sand beaches along the surf on both the Atlantic and Pacific coasts, are caught by hand or with special scoop traps. They are used for such fish as striped bass, bonefish, sheepshead, tautog, and pompano along the East Coast and for corbina and croakers along the West Coast.

When it comes to salt-water minnows or bait fish, you have some of the most effective baits which can be used for the game fish of the sea. There are many kinds, such as mullet, menhaden, sand eels, spearing or silversides, herring, anchovies, sardines, candlefish, killifish, mackerel, bonito, flying fish, needlefish, balaos, blue runners and small sea catfish. The big bait fish are rigged whole and are trolled for sailfish, marlin, swordfish and tuna. The bait fish can also be cut into triangular strips of varying lengths for this purpose. Strips and chunks cut from the larger bait fish can be used for bottom fishing or drifted in the current.

The smaller bait fish are used dead or alive, and are hooked through the lips, eye, gills or back, for many game fish.

The most important thing to remember when using bait fish is to keep them alive or use only fresh ones. Dead bait fish or stale bait fish are not as effective.

14

Fishing Streams, Rivers and Lakes

THE MERE POSSESSION of a spinning outfit doesn't assure you of catching fish. Many a beginner has been rudely awakened to this fact after he has bought a spin rod, reel, line and lures, and has gone to the nearest body of water to try them out. He quickly notices that he can cast light lures farther than he ever could before. But he also discovers that casting alone doesn't make him a much better fisherman than he formerly was. It helps him reach distant spots he could not reach with other outfits and he can use many new, light lures he couldn't handle before. But it is somewhat of a shock to learn that many other fishermen still using the older outfits catch more fish than he does with his brand-new spinning outfit.

Anyone who has been fishing for any length of time soon realizes that he has many things to learn. The type of fishing tackle you use is important and can play a big part in angling success. But in the long run the angler who knows fish habits, where to find fish, how to approach them, how to present and work a lure or bait has the biggest advantage. Such an angler will be successful on more occasions, regardless of the tackle used. So even though the spinning outfit is the most versatile and boulders present or visible in a fast run there are still many feed-

143

deadly fishing tackle yet developed, you still have to study the waters you fish, the fish themselves, where they hide and feed, how to work the lure to make them hit and, finally, how to play and land them.

Fresh-water spin fishing is done in brooks, streams, rivers, ponds and lakes. Of all these, the hardest waters to fish are the small brooks and streams. And the fish found there, usually some member of the trout family, are among the hardest to catch. This is only natural, since the water in the streams is generally clear and trout are wary fish. The slightest disturbance in the water or a falling shadow will scare the fish.

So the way you approach such waters is very important. In the smaller streams, wading through the water should be avoided. No matter how slowly and carefully you wade you usually send ripples or bump stones, which alarms the fish. Do your fishing from shore and hide behind the brush or tree trunks if you can. If no cover is available, get down low in a crouch or even on your knees. A slow, deliberate approach is always better than rushing up to the stream bank. It is often possible to get within easy fishing distance of a trout even in clear, shallow water if you inch your way a little at a time and avoid fast movements of the hands or body. Cast with a wrist and hand movement only.

If you do have to wade in the stream itself, do so as quietly as possible. When you reach a favorable position, stop and stay there. The less walking and moving around you do the better.

The biggest problem is to locate the fish, so that you know exactly where to cast. Natives who live along the stream or anglers who fish there often naturally have the advantage. They know through past experience just where the fish can be found, and don't waste time fishing in unproductive spots. Of course, sometimes trout can be seen lying on the bottom or swimming around. Or they may be rising to the surface to feed on flies and other insects.

However, most of the time you don't see the fish and have to

Catfish like this big bullhead provide top sport on spinning tackle.

Not too long ago bass like this were caught mostly on bait-casting tackle. Today it's spinning gear that does the trick.

Most lakes are best fished from a boat. And wilderness lakes, like this one in Glacier National Park, Montana, call for rubber boats which can be toted through the woods.

Spinning tackle is highly adaptable to small streams or big rivers. Here the angler plays a steelhead.

fish blind, casting into spots where a fish may be lying or feeding. That is when the ability to "read" the water pays off.

Trout like clean, cold water. Some streams are better in this respect than others. A good trout stream will contain many fish in a relatively small area. Brook trout like the coldest water and are usually found mostly in our northern states and Canada at the higher altitudes. Rainbow trout also like cold waters, but can live in somewhat warmer waters than brook trout. The brown trout is the most adaptable and can live in warmer waters than can the other two.

But no matter which species of trout, they all have the same basic requirements. First is the matter of survival; trout seek protection in those parts of a stream where their enemies can't find them. So when they are not actively feeding you'll find trout hiding under rocks, sunken logs, tree trunks, roots, ledges and undercut banks.

Trout are fast, powerful swimmers, but they don't like to buck the current all day long. So when they hide they also pick spots where the water is quiet or the current is weak. Most of their hiding places offer such resting spots.

However, when a trout gets hungry he must often leave his hiding or resting spot and either swim around searching for food or pick a location where the current brings the food to him. That is when he is most active and will take a properly presented lure or bait. When a trout is hiding or resting he can also be made to strike, but it usually takes more effort and the bait or lure must be offered right in front of his nose to interest him. When actively feeding, a trout will often go out of his way a few feet to hit a lure or bait.

The best feeding areas are found where the shallow riffles enter a pool. A deep, fast run among rocks and boulders also creates good trout water. Here trout will be found lying in front of the boulder, along its sides and behind it. Where there are no ing spots which can be fished. Wherever there's a deeper spot or hole in such a run a trout can lie comfortably on the bottom. These are often revealed by the darker color of the water.

Another good spot in a stream is alongside deep-cut banks and undercut banks. Here the trout lie alongside or under the banks and wait for drifting food swept by the current or for an insect to come falling in from the shore itself.

Many stream anglers pass up the shallow ends of the pools. It's true that these are harder to fish and many times are barren of trout, but there are other times when trout come there to feed on underwater insects such as nymphs, or to chase minnows. These shallow waters are often good in the late afternoon, evening and at night.

The deep pools themselves often contain many trout but these spots are usually heavily fished by anglers. The trout are often wary and hard to hook. They also have plenty of time to look a lure over and aren't in a hurry to take it. When they are actively feeding on top, rising for fly hatches, they will often strike a properly presented dry fly. But most of the time the trout will be near the bottom and the lure or bait must be offered there for best results. Pool fishing is generally best early in the season and late in the season and also during the hot summer months when streams are very low.

The stream spin fisherman should carry a good assortment of lures for trout and know how to use them. One of the best is the small, wobbling spoon. Choose the smallest and lightest you can find. They are especially effective in the deeper runs, pools and quieter waters. You can get them down near the bottom, where other lures fail to reach. A spoon can be cast across the stream and then allowed to swing with the current as it sinks. Not much action is needed at this time, just a tight line and an occasional turn of the reel handle to take up any slack. When the lure reaches a point directly downstream an erratic retrieve is started with regular raising and lowering of the rod tip which allows the lure to rise and then sink and flutter down again.

She's holding a 13½-pound rainbow trout caught through the ice on spinning tackle and 6-lb. test line.

Here's a beauty of a steelhead taken on spinning tackle.

These Florida bass are big, but spinning tackle can handle them.

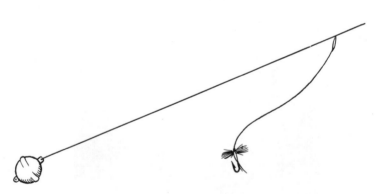

Using a fly with a plastic float.

In the deeper pools you must let the spoon sink almost to the bottom and work it back very slowly, with occasional jerks of the rod tip to make it flash and dance off the bottom. If you have trouble getting down to the bottom, try casting the lure across and well upstream, so that it sinks deeper. Naturally you're going to lose an occasional spoon when it fouls on the bottom, but you'll also catch more and bigger fish.

The spinners with revolving blades around a shaft are also good trout lures for stream fishing. Here again the lightest and smallest ones are usually the most effective. They can be fished in the same ways as the wobbling spoon by casting across stream and letting them swing and sink with the current. They can also be fished in other ways, such as casting them directly downstream and retrieving them slowly through likely looking spots. If the lure reaches a pocket where a fish may be lying it can be held there for a while and worked back and forth almost in the same spot until you get a strike. This, of course, works only in fairly fast water and with light spinners.

Another way to fish light spinners is to cast them upstream and reel them back as fast as you can past the hiding places of big trout. On certain days a slower retrieve will work but most of the time fast reeling will bring strikes. For this you need a spinning reel with a fast retrieve.

Spoons and spinners work best early and late in the season, when the water is cold and there are no fly hatches. But they are always good for big trout, which feed mostly on minnows and small fish.

Streamers and bucktails are also effective lures, especially for the larger trout. You can use weighted ones made especially for spinning, but the unweighted ones are also deadly if used with a spit shot or two or small clincher on the leader. They can also be used with the regular fly lines or the short fly lines which are attached to the end of the monofilament line. Streamers are deadly toward dusk and when trout are chasing minnows. They also take many fish when the water gets "milky" or slightly brown after a recent rain.

When trout are rising to the surface to feed on flies you can take them on dry flies. One method is to use the regular mono line and tie one of the plastic floats on the end. Then the fly is tied about 3 ft. above the float on a short dropper leader. The bubble lands with a splash and often frightens the trout, but on other occasions it doesn't, and they will rise and take the fly. For best results cast the bubble so that it lands well above and slightly beyond the fishing area. Then let the fly float down toward the fish. This method is best on the larger streams and rivers.

You can also use a regular fly reel and line on your spinning rod and do a pretty good job of casting flies. You can cast dry flies, wet flies, nymphs and streamers without any added weight. And you can use a long, tapered leader at the end of the fly line. The important thing is to get a floating fly line heavy enough to cast with the spinning rod you use. You can put this on a small fly reel and carry it in your bag or pocket until needed. Then when trout start feeding on dry flies, wet flies or nymphs you are ready for them. Dry flies, of course, float on top of the water and imitate the adult insect. Wet flies simulate drowned insects or those rising to the surface to hatch. They are fished underwater at varying depths. Flies should be carried in various sizes and patterns, depending on the locality being fished.

The stream fisherman will find that there are times when natural baits are better than artificial lures. This is especially true when the trout season opens in the spring and streams are high, cold and usually roily. At such times trout aren't very active and lie on the bottom. A worm drifted slowly along the bottom, however, will often be taken by such fish.

When using a small angleworm you may need a split shot or two above the hook to cast out far enough and get the worm down deep enough in the fast current. A night crawler can be cast quite a distance without weight, but if the current is strong you may need some split shot to sink it to the bottom.

Sometimes a small Colorado or other spinner, baited with a small worm, works better than a plain worm. Here you can also drift the worm with the current, with slight twitches of the rod tip, and also work it back against the current at the end of the drift.

Worms are also good later in the season after a shower or rain raises the level of the stream and makes the water slightly brown. At such times big trout often start feeding. A night crawler or earthworm drifted through deep runs and heads of pools will be taken by fish which wouldn't look at the same bait in clear, low water.

Minnows will also take trout, especially big cannibal fish which want a good mouthful. Here minnows between 2 and 3 in. in length are best. Trout will take a dead minnow, and they are easier and more fun to use than a live one. The minnow is sewed on the hook either headfirst or tailfirst on the leader. When fishing the minnow let it drift and tumble downstream with the current. Sometimes a trout will hit a minnow that is being drawn upstream against the current. These minnows are usually given a curve so that they revolve.

Other baits which can be used for big trout are crayfish and frogs, which can be cast without any sinker or weight. Smaller baits, such as hellgrammites, nymphs, grasshoppers, grubs, caterpillars and beetles, can be fished with the plastic float or bobber. Here the float should be put on the leader about 3 or 4 ft. above the hook. For best results cast upstream and let the bait drift naturally with the current.

If you plan to do a lot of bait fishing you'll find the longer, more flexible spinning rods best for this work. They make it easier to cast the softer and lighter baits without snapping them off. And the longer rod makes it possible to work and manipulate the baits better in the water.

The spin angler fishing larger river waters can often use the same lures and techniques for such fish as trout as described for stream fishing. Only here you have to contend with stronger currents, deeper and broader waters. The fish are usually larger, also, and heavier lures and sinkers are often used. So the river spin fisherman often has to use somewhat longer, heavier and stronger rods to handle the big fish and lures which may be used. Such rods also help make the longer casts needed to reach the best fishing spots. This often calls for the larger fresh-water spinning reels or smaller salt-water models to be used with the heavier rod.

There are three main ways to fish a big river. From shore, by wading or from a boat. If the river is too deep to wade and you have no boat, your only choice is shore fishing. Here you can often fish without boots, but they can be worn if the shore line is muddy. In rivers with shallow bars and gradually sloping shores you can use boots to wade out a short distance from shore. But on most big rivers waders are needed to reach the best fishing spots.

Most of the big-trout rivers are in the West and the rainbow trout is the most common in these waters. Rainbows, especially the big ones, like deep, swift water with scattered rocks and boulders where they can lie and rest. Such water can be fished by casting at various angles, so that every hole, pocket and boulder is covered. Another good spot for trout in big rivers is at the foot of riffles, where they enter a pool.

When fishing big rivers for trout it is usually best to keep moving and cover as much water as possible. Of course, you should fish each good spot thoroughly. But the more territory you cover the better chance you have of locating fish. Once located, however, the slow, methodical coverage of the spots is best.

Spoons are excellent lures for trout in rivers. They sink deep and reach the fish lying on the bottom, even in the deepest pools and runs. The thicker, heavier spoons usually work best in deep waters. The spinners are better for the shallower waters and for fishing across and downstream in likely looking spots. Because of the big trout present in many large rivers, small plugs often work well. These can be cast across and upstream, then reeled slowly and steadily.

Trout in rivers also feed on insects and dry flies; wet flies and nymphs can also be fished with the plastic float or bubble. If the fish are close, a fly line can be used with the spinning rod. Trout in rivers will also take a great variety of natural baits, such as minnows and worms.

The sea-going rainbow — the steelhead — has always been a popular fish with Northwest anglers in California, Oregon, Washington and British Columbia. Steelhead fishermen really took to spinning tackle in a big way. When you use spin tackle for these gamesters you have a big advantage over other tackle. You can cast farther, work your lure or bait deeper and fight the fish in a sporting manner.

The steelhead enter the rivers from the ocean on their spawning runs upstream. Although steelhead will enter fresh-water rivers almost every month of the year, two periods offer peak fishing. One is the summer run and the other, the winter run. The exact time of the runs depends on weather and water conditions, and the confirmed steelhead angler keeps in close touch with the situation on his favorite river. The local tackle dealer can usually give you some good dope on the river in his area.

In any given steelhead river certain pools and runs are better than others. Even in the pool itself certain spots are chosen by the fish for resting and feeding. The natives and old-timers know these spots from past experience and work their lures or baits so that the fish see them. The beginner or stranger is handicapped by lack of this knowledge. But there are general locations and preferences of steelhead which will help an angler to locate these fish.

Steelhead like fast, deep runs, and there they choose some

obstruction, such as a sunken boulder, log or hole, where they lie to avoid the full force of the current. In pools they are found in the tails or lower ends, where they rest. When they are on the move again they lie at the head of the pool. Most of the time they stay in or near the main channels.

When rivers are very low steelhead fishing falls off. When the water starts to rise fishing usually improves. If the water gets too high and muddy the fishing gets poor again.

Steelhead will take a variety of lures and baits. The smaller fish found in the rivers during the summer are more active and will rise to flies, spinners and spoons. Lighter spinning rods and reels can be used at this time.

For winter fishing you need somewhat heavier rods and a larger reel in order to cope with strong currents, bigger fish and heavier lures and sinkers. Here, for best results, you have to work your lure or bait deep, almost on the bottom. When the water isn't too muddy, spoons and spinners such as the "cherry bobber" are effective. When the water gets roily, natural baits such as salmon eggs, night crawlers and crayfish tails are better. To get such lures or baits down deep they usually have to be weighted with split shot or clamp-on sinkers on the leader about 2 ft. above the bait or lure. Other rigs make use of a small dropper leader to which a sinker is tied or squeezed on.

No matter which lure or bait you use, the secret is to make it bump slowly along the bottom until it hits a steelie almost on the nose. You have to be alert for the slightest pick-up or hit indicating the fish has taken the lure or bait. It pays to attempt to set the hook when you feel such pick-ups, even if in doubt.

Steelhead fishing is often cold, wet and miserable during the winter months; but the minute you hook a fish you forget all the discomfort, and the excitement warms you up in a hurry. Few fish found in our fresh waters fight harder than a good-sized steelhead. And for the most thrills and fun, use the lightest spinning rod, reel and line that is practical for the fishing at hand.

In many of the northwestern steelhead rivers you can also catch salmon in the fresh-water portions of the river. Two kinds of salmon are usually caught: the big chinook or king salmon and smaller silver salmon. The same spinning tackle used for steelhead will also work for salmon. In waters where big "kings" are expected, heavier rods, reels and lines can be used.

Salmon will take spinners, spoons, small plugs and salmon eggs. The heavier sinking lures can be used without added weight, but the lighter buoyant spinners, plugs and baits require small sinkers on the leader to get the lure down deep, where it can drift and bump along the bottom.

Another river favorite with spinning anglers is the scrappy small-mouth bass. Small-mouth black bass may be found in many places in a river—cruising along the shore line, in deep pools or in riffles. They like a place they can call home, and hang around sunken logs and trees, boulders, under ledges or undercut banks. When feeding they may cruise around over rock bars and points. Generally they come into the shallow water in the evening or at night.

When they are in these shallow waters such lures as weighted bass bugs, streamers and small surface plugs are good lures to use.

In the deeper pools or faster runs a spoon or weighted spinner is better. These are worked behind the boulders, through the eddies and the pockets. They are also cast out into the deeper pools across and upstream and allowed to drift down, with occasional sweeps of the rod tip to make the lure dart and tumble.

The river small-mouth often falls for such natural baits as worms, minnows, crayfish and hellgrammites. Worms can be drifted with the current naturally or they can be fished with a float or on the bottom with a sinker. When using the smaller worms for still fishing, several on a hook are often better than one.

Minnows can be used dead or alive. The dead ones are best for drifting in the riffles or fast runs, while live ones are used for still fishing in the pools.

The crayfish is a natural food of small-mouth bass and therefore a top bait, especially in rivers or streams where they are plentiful and known to be eaten by the fish. The soft-shelled crayfish are preferred, but a hard one will also take bass. It should be fished on the bottom, where the fish look for them crawling over the rocks.

The hellgrammite is also eaten with relish by river small-mouths. They can be drifted in the shallow parts of the river or fished deep on the bottom, with a small sinker in the deeper pools.

Whichever bait you use for small-mouth bass, give them plenty of time to take and swallow it. When the fish can be seen, wait until the bait disappears in his mouth and he starts to move away. When fishing blind, wait until the float or line starts moving away at a fast rate.

In many of the rivers where small-mouth bass are found you'll also find the walleye. They like the deep pools and eddies, especially where the river cuts into the shore and gouges out a deep hole. They also come into shallow waters at dusk and at night. Walleyes bite best in, the spring and fall. They'll take a wide variety of lures, such as spoons, spinners, underwater plugs, weighted flies and jigs, when cast with spin tackle. The thing to remember is to reel slowly, for walleyes rarely take a fast-moving lure. Slow trolling with spinner and worm or minnow combinations is also deadly. And they will take live minnows fished deep, especially in the daytime when lures fail to interest them. Although walleyes come big, they don't fight quite as hard as the top fresh-water game fish; so light or medium weight spinning rods will do the trick.

The shad is a wonderful light-tackle fish and can be caught in some rivers along both the Atlantic and Pacific Coasts. The light or ultralight spinning rod is made to order for them. However, they are usually found in fast currents and a somewhat heavier rod and line will enable you to handle the fish better against the current.

On the East Coast such rivers as the Susquehanna, Delaware, Connecticut, James, Potomac and St. John's have big shad runs, and fishing for them is great sport. The best months in the northern rivers are from April to June. In Florida's St. John they are caught in January and February.

On the West Coast, where shad were introduced in 1871, they have spread out from Southern California to as far north as Alaska. The heaviest concentrations are in the San Francisco Bay and Coos Bay areas and in the tributaries of the Columbia River.

Shad strike best in fast water, and channels are favorite spots. They also congregate in pools and eddies, where they can often be seen flashing underwater.

The best lures for shad are small hooks wrapped with shiny foil, and small bright-yellow, white or red wet flies and streamers. Small spinners and spoons are also good. These are presented either from shore or from an anchored boat. Trolling often works, too. Shad may hit anywhere from a couple of feet below the surface down to the bottom, so it's important to find the level they are hitting at. From an anchored boat in a fast current it is often necessary to add a sinker of one or two ounces on the end of the line. Then tie the lure about 3 ft. above it on a $3\frac{1}{2}$-ft. leader. This is "worked" back along the bottom from an anchored boat with the help of a fast current.

A shad on the end of the line is a fast bundle of energy and power, and will run and leap all over the place. They should be played with care since they have tender mouths. You'll lose plenty of fish no matter how carefully you play them, however. A big landing net is a help when boating them.

The catfishes provide a lot of sport, fun and food for fresh-water river anglers all over the country. The smaller varieties, especially the bullheads and channel catfish, put up a good scrap on light spinning tackle. Bullheads like a gob of worms on a hook, and in quiet waters they can be fished without a sinker. In strong currents a small sinker must be used. The channel cat will also take worms, but live or dead minnows are often used. Channel cats have also been known to strike slow-moving artificial lures at times.

For the larger catfish, such as the blue catfish and the flathead catfish, you can use the light or medium outfits when they are running small. But when you go after the big ones you'll need the heavier fresh-water or even salt-water spinning rods and heavy lines. They take many baits, such as worms, minnows, small fish, hunks of meat and stink baits. The bait must be fished down deep or on the bottom. Night fishing is usually most productive for catfish.

Another fish often found in the larger, sluggish rivers is the carp. Here's a fish often overlooked or neglected by anglers. But he's a real powerhouse when hooked on light tackle, and on a spin outfit a big carp will give you a workout you won't forget.

It also requires quite a bit of patience to hook a big, smart carp. They take their time about swallowing a bait. So don't strike until you see the line moving off at a fast pace.

Carp like the quieter sections of rivers, especially if the bottom is muddy and covered with water plants. They grub along the bottom with their big lips picking up tidbits. The best bait is usually a doughball made of equal parts of flour and corn meal. Some sugar or honey is usually added to this and then it is molded around a hook. If carp are small in the water you are fishing use No. 2 or No. 1 hooks, but for the larger ones use 2/0 or 3/0 hooks. The Eagle Claw is a good hook pattern for them. Carp will also take fresh- or canned-corn kernels, green peas, lima beans and parboiled potatoes. All of these should be fished on the bottom for best results. A sinker may be used to cast out and also hold the bait on the bottom in a current.

When fishing lakes, ponds and reservoirs it is often even more difficult to locate the fish than it is in rivers. Some lakes and reservoirs are big bodies of water, and you can waste a lot of time fishing the wrong spots.

In general, fish found in lakes have the same needs as stream or river fish; they want food and a safe hiding place. So you will find most of them in areas where they can find plenty of food or where they can take cover from their enemies. They also require enough oxygen in the water for comfortable living, and most fish like shady spots or deep water where they can avoid the bright sun. There are exceptions, of course, such as sunfish and a few others. But most game fish usually hide from the sun and from enemies and lurk unseen so that they can surprise a small fish, frog or other creature. They also move into deeper or cooler water when the water near shore or at the surface gets too warm.

To locate the best fishing spots in most lakes will require a knowledge of water depths and the type of bottom found there. This knowledge can be obtained by studying lake survey maps and charts, by making soundings with lead weights or even by skin diving and studying the depths and bottoms. All this dope will come in useful later on when you want to fish various spots in case the first ones fail to produce.

Of all the fish found in lakes the large-mouth black bass is easily the top favorite. He has been introduced in most of our states, and is found in the smallest ponds and the largest reservoirs and lakes. He grows fairly large, fights hard and can be taken on a variety of lures and baits. Most important, the bass is a smart fish compared to some of the others. A big bass that has been "educated" by being hooked or fooled a few times often offers a challenge that no true angler can resist. More plugs and other large lures have been designed to fool bass than any other fish.

The usual procedure when fishing for large-mouth bass from a boat is to row slowly, within casting distance from shore, and cast your lure into likely looking spots. This is usually best very early in the morning and toward dusk. Also, if you care to fish at night, a surface plug is one of the best lures to use at this time. Such lures as a popper, gurgler or swimmer, which throw a splash or make a commotion when jerked or reeled, are the best to use. To get results, fish slowly, allowing the lure to rest motionless at the end of the cast, then twitching or jerking it, letting it rest again, then jerking it again, and so on until the lure is near the boat. There are times, however, when bass will take a fast-moving surface plug, usually when they are chasing minnows.

When the bass refuse the larger surface plugs, the smaller, lighter-weight spinning bugs or bass bugs will often work. These are fished in much the same way as the surface plugs except that instead of imitating a minnow or small fish you should try to simulate the crippled actions of a small frog, moth, beetle or other insect.

If the bass aren't near shore try fishing a few feet deep and some distance from shore. Here the diving underwater plugs will often do the trick. These can be retrieved steadily or with a stop and go action. Spoons can also be used, and these also work best when retrieved erratically. A strip of pork rind can be added to the spoon if the plain one doesn't produce.

Deep-water bass are very partial to live baits fished on or near the bottom. Large-mouths often take gobs of worms or two or three big night crawlers on the hook. Sometimes a single night crawler, hooked once, will also work. Or a minnow hooked through the back is allowed to swim around down deep. You may need a small clincher on the leader, to get the minnow down, but in most cases try to avoid sinkers or other weights when using live baits.

Another excellent live bait for large-mouths is a small, lively frog. They can be fished near shore or around lily pads on the surface by allowing them to move about. Or they can be fished near the bottom, with a light sinker. Other baits, such as crickets and grasshoppers, can also be used. With a spinning outfit you can, of course, cast the heavier baits way out without added weight. The lighter baits can be fished with plastic floats or bobbers to provide casting weight or to keep the bait above the weeds or bottom.

The whole trick in bait fishing for bass is to use lively baits, keep them moving and let the fish swallow them before setting the hook.

If you'd rather use artificial lures for bass when they are down deep you'll find the sinking underwater plugs, jigs and plastic worms are the best lures to use. These are allowed to sink to the bottom and are then worked slowly, in short jerks and twitches.

Another popular lake or pond fish in the eastern part of the country is the pickerel. They are found from Ontario to Florida in small ponds, lakes and sluggish parts of rivers. Pickerel like small plugs, but one of the best lures is a red-and-white painted spoon or a weighted spinner fished along the edges of weeds or lily pads. These fish also take streamers or bucktails. For live bait you can't beat a small minnow.

The big brother of the pickerel is the pike which has many of the same trait of lying under lily pads or among weeds, waiting for some small fish to come by. However, pike come much bigger than pickerel, and while a light spinning outfit is ideal for the smaller pickerel, a medium or heavy outfit is better for pike, not only because of the size and power of a big pike but also because you cast larger lures and baits.

The best place to catch pike is in Canada. If you can't go there, then fish our northern states and areas, such as the Great Lakes Region of Wisconsin, Michigan and Minnesota. The best time of the year to go after them is in the spring and fall, then they will often bite throughout the day. During the summer you may have to fish early in the morning and in the evening or when it is cloudy or raining.

In shallow waters a surface plug will often raise a pike, especially in the morning or in the evening. Later in the day an underwater plug often produces. A good-sized spoon or spinner can also be used. While casting takes many fish, trolling with these lures covers more territory and increases your chances.

When pike refuse artificial lures a big minnow or a small fish, such as a sucker or yellow perch, will often tempt them.

If pike are too small for you, you can take a crack at the biggest member of the pike family — the muskellunge. They are found in many of the same waters and places as the pike. But they are usually more scattered and like bigger bodies of waters, so you often have to locate a fish first before you can try for him. That is why trolling, which enables you to cover more territory, usually takes many muskies year in and year out.

You can use many of the same lures and baits for muskies that are used for pike. Big surface and underwater plugs, spoons and spinners with large bucktails, for example. A heavy fresh-water spinning rod or a light salt-water spinning rod should be used for these fish. The largest fresh-water spinning reels or smaller-sized salt-water reels are used with these rods. Lines testing from 8 to 15 lbs. are used with such outfits. A wire leader at least 20 or 30 in. long is required if you want to hold the muskies after they are hooked.

Set the hook hard, especially when fishing with lures. Muskies have tough jaws. When using live baits, such as suckers, give a muskie plenty of time to swallow the bait. In muskie fishing perseverance and determination will pay off more than in most types of fishing. You have to keep going out day after day, week after week and month after month.

One of the gamest fish found in lakes is the landlocked salmon. Their speed and wild leaps will delight the light-tackle spin fisherman no end. Unfortunately, they are not too well distributed, being found mostly in parts of New York state, New England and Canada. A few lakes are also being stocked as far south as New Jersey, but in general landlocked salmon prefer colder, deeper northern waters.

For real thrills, the expert angler will use the light spinning rod and 4 or 6-lb. test line. The beginner will be safer with the medium or heavy spin rod and 8 or 10-lb. test line until he gets skilled at playing the fish.

The landlocked salmon takes streamer flies, such as the Supervisor, Gray Ghost and Green Ghost, as well as spinners, spoons or small plugs. The time-honored method is to troll close to shore or around the mouths of streams entering the lake, where the salmon feed on smelt and other small fish. Two rods can be used —one can have a streamer fly about 50 or 60 feet behind the boat, while the other rod can have a small spoon about 30 feet or so behind. The boat should move at a fairly fast speed, say 4 or 6 miles per hour.

You can also anchor the boat or drift near shore or around the mouths of streams, over weed beds or rocky bars, and cast small spoons to take salmon. The best fishing takes place early in the spring, as soon as the ice is out. At this time the hungry salmon swarm into the shallow water to feed on minnows and small fish. Later, when the water warms up, they go deeper and spoons or spinners must be trolled way down to get them.

Another fish often found in the same waters or same areas as the landlocked salmon is the lake trout. However, the spin angler has only a short period when he can get this fish on light tackle. That also occurs early in the spring, when the ice is out, and later on in the fall. In between these times, the lake trout go deep, and then heavy tackle is required to get them, with wire lines and conventional rods and reels preferred. Unless, of course, you can make a trip to Alaska, where lake trout (or mackinaws as they are called) feed more on the surface throughout the summer months.

When these fish can be taken on top, a medium spinning rod that can cast spoons and plugs provides plenty of sport. Lake trout are found mostly in New England, the Great Lakes region, Canada and Alaska. When they come close to shore you can get them by casting or trolling. Try working the lure at different depths until you find the level the fish are feeding at.

Many of the trout found in streams and rivers also live in lakes, where they often grow to lunker size and make worth-while trophies. And even the smaller trout provide plenty of sport on an ultralight or light spinning outfit. The brook trout, for example, grows much bigger when found in large lakes than in small streams or brooks. Although the brookie has been stocked in many of our northern streams and lakes, he's most numerous in Maine and in Ontario, Quebec and New Brunswick in Canada.

The light spinning rod and line are best for these native trout, and you can use a wide variety of lures, such as small spoons in various finishes, spinners, spinner-fly combinations, streamers and wet flies.

Rainbow trout of the lakes grow to monster size and many are caught each year on spinning tackle, especially in our western lakes. The most famous body of water is Pend Oreille Lake in Idaho, where a 37 lb. rainbow was taken on conventional tackle. But other fish close to that weight have been taken on spinning tackle. There are many other lakes in our northern and western states and in Canada where big rainbows are caught. Rainbows of the lakes stay in deep water during the summer months, when trolling with wire lines or weighted lines is often done in the larger lakes, to get to the proper depths. Conventional tackle is usually more satisfactory for this work, but in the early spring the big rainbows will come to the surface and close to shore, especially around the mouths of streams and rivers entering the lakes. Then they can often be taken by casting or trolling spoons, small plugs, spinners or streamer flies. These big trout usually feed on some kind of minnow or small fish, so lures resembling these are best. However, they will also take wet flies, nymphs and dry flies at times, usually late in the evening when insects are hatching or are active over the water.

Another western trout often found in lakes is the cutthroat, which also reaches a large size in such waters. The Rocky Mountain region has the best fishing for these fish. They are wonderful fish to take on dry flies, especially in streams and rivers. But the larger cutthroat found in lakes usually prefer a spoon, spinner or small plug, trolled fairly deep.

The Dolly Varden trout is also found in many of the same waters and areas as the cutthroat trout. Those found in lakes often reach a much bigger size than the ones in streams. Here they are caught by trolling fairly deep with spoons, spinners and plugs. They also take live baits such as minnows and small fish. In streams and rivers the Dolly Varden is notorious as an eater of salmon eggs and these make good bait.

Now we come to the most popular group of fishes caught in lakes — the pan fishes. These small but numerous fishes are far easier to catch than the so-called game fishes, and millions of anglers seek them. The old stand-by for years has been the cane pole with a bobber or float. But it's much more fun to catch them on a light spinning outfit. And if you really want to get the most out of this fishing try catching panfish on an ultralight spin rod with a line testing only a pound or two. With this you can cast tiny lures or bait, and even a small pan fish will surprise you with the scrap he puts up.

One of the best artificial lures for bluegills, or bream as they are called down south, is a small bass bug. You can cast one of these if you attach a fly reel to your spin rod and use a fly line. With regular monofilament line you can add a small cork or tiny surface plug a foot or so ahead of the bass bug, to give you casting weight. Actually you use "pan fish" bugs, since these are smaller than bass bugs and are made specially for pan fish.

This bug is worked very slowly. After you cast, just let it lie there a minute or so, then slowly twitch it and pull it a few inches. Then let it rest again, twitch it and reel it in once more a few inches. If there are any bluegills or other large sunfish around they'll come up and take it. They'll also take a dry fly fished with a fly line or a plastic float. Sunfish will also go for tiny streamers, spoons, spinners and plugs.

Of course, there is also that old favorite for sunfish—the worm. These should be small garden worms instead of night crawlers. Sunfish have small mouths and you'll miss too many with big worms. Small No. 6 or No. 8 hooks should also be used. Sunfish will also take crickets, grasshoppers, beetles, grubs and meal worms on a hook.

Another popular pan fish is the yellow perch. Perch are school fish and where there's one there are usually more. Large catches of yellow perch are common in waters where they are plentiful. However, fish in a lake, which has mostly big ones. In some waters yellow perch never reach a big size. Yellow perch like the larger, deeper lakes where they are found over submerged weeds, rock or gravel bars, around pilings, docks and bridges.

Perch will take small spinners, spinner-and-worm combinations, tiny plugs, spoons and flies. But one of the best baits is a small minnow fished deep. Minnows from $1\frac{1}{2}$ to 2 in. are the best sizes to use. The biggest perch are usually down deep, so you'll have to fish without a float and may have to add a split shot or two, to get your minnow down.

Another school pan fish found in many of our larger lakes and reservoirs is the white bass. They often come to the surface in large numbers, to chase and feed on small minnows. They churn the water to a froth and are easy to locate at such times. You can race over with your boat, cut the motor and cast a small spoon, surface or shallow-running plug or a small jig into the school and reel it through the commotion. Action will usually be fast as long as they stay on top. When they stop showing, you can often take them by using a deep-running or sinking lure. They also take live minnows fished deep.

The crappies, both the white and black kinds, are also popular pan fish, and are a lot of fun to catch on light or ultralight spinning tackle. They also tend to school up, and big catches are possible. Although crappies will sometimes hit small spoons, plugs, spinners and jigs, a live minnow is one of the best baits to use for them. Look for crappies close to weeds, lily pads, hyacinths, etc.

These are the most important fresh-water fish caught in lakes, streams and rivers. But there are others, and almost any fresh-water species can be caught on spinning tackle. It is just a question of matching the proper rod, reel, line and lures to the fishing to be done.

15

Salt-water Inshore Spinning

FOR MANY KINDS of salt-water fishing the spinning outfit has been replacing the conventional fishing outfits. This is especially true along our inshore waters, where casting lures for the smaller and medium-sized game fish and bottom fish is the common practice. Today you'll find spin anglers fishing the tidal rivers, bays, sounds, inlets and other inshore waters. And they are catching fish by casting from shore, boats, piers and bridges and by trolling. The same versatility which makes the spinning outfit so popular in fresh-water fishing also carries over into salt water.

Let's look at some of the salt-water fish being caught in inshore waters, and how it is being done. One of the most popular fish on both the East and West Coasts is the striped bass. Many of these fish are taken from the surf by spin casters. This will be covered in the following chapter on spinning in the surf. Here we are mainly concerned with striper fishing in the rivers, bays and other inshore protected waters.

Along the Atlantic Coast the smaller stripers are numerous at the present time, and spin anglers are making good catches from shore and boats. Stripers like fast water when feeding and gather around piers, bridges and trestles, where they lie waiting for the current to wash some tidbit their way or for a small fish to swim by. They also range over tidal flats, rips, channels and creeks, often feeding early in the morning, in the evening and at night. When they are chasing small fish they attract seagulls or can be seen breaking water.

These stripers are taken by spin anglers casting small metal squids, spoons, plugs and jigs, which are allowed to swing with the tide and then are reeled back in a jerk-and-pause technique. Slow trolling with the same lures or spinner-worm combinations also accounts for many stripers. If lures fail, bait fishing with bloodworms, sandworms or clamworms, soft-shell or shedder crabs, squid or small bait fish will often take them. If the current isn't too strong these baits can be drifted with or without a float. However, most of the time the baits should be fished near the bottom on a three-foot leader tied to the main fishing line. Spin anglers can find stripers along the Atlantic Coast from Nova Scotia to Florida. Fishing is usually best from April to November.

Along the Pacific Coast striped-bass fishing is done in such areas as the bays, rivers and sloughs near San Francisco in California and in Coos Bay, Oregon. Stripers can often be taken all year in California waters. They get slow and sluggish during the winter months, but some big fish can be taken at this time. But the peak fishing takes place in the spring and again in the fall.

The majority of the stripers taken on the West Coast fall for natural baits such as sardines, anchovies, herring or some other small fish. The sardine is the most popular, and is used fresh or frozen. It is cut into chunks or strips and is used on a long 3 or 4-ft. leader above a sinker heavy enough to hold in the current. For big striped bass a live sculpin or bullhead is a top bait.

When West-Coast stripers come into the shallows or can be seen chasing and feeding on bait fish they can often be taken by casting and trolling. The most popular lures are spoons, underwater plugs and jigs, often used in combinations of two on the same line.

Spinning anglers along the Atlantic Coast have been having

wonderful sport with bluefish in recent years. However, it won't be long before these fish will disappear from our waters, so the time to enjoy this fishing is right now. The smaller blues come into the inlets, bays and along the beaches, where they can be caught by trolling with metal squids, jigs and rubber-tube lures. Spoons are also good for them, as well as most shiny-metal lures. When bluefish chase bait fish on the surface great sport can be had by casting small surface popping plugs, metal squids, spoons or jigs among them.

In certain areas the most popular and effective method of catching bluefish is by chumming with ground menhaden or "bunker" from an anchored or drifting boat. This brings them near the boat, where a hook of 7/0 or 8/0 size is baited with a chunk of bunker or butterfish and is drifted out with the tide.

The smaller blues average from 1 to 3lbs. and these are usually caught in inshore waters. For them a light spinning outfit with about 6 or 8-lb. test line is ideal. The larger blues caught along the beaches or in deeper offshore water may run from 4 to 15 lbs. For them a medium spinning outfit with a 12 or 15-lb. test line is more practical.

A top sport fish which can be taken by spin anglers along the Pacific Coast is the salmon. They run up the fresh-water rivers to spawn, but can be taken in salt water along the coast in inshore waters and in the inlets, river mouths and bays. The best-known and most popular is the mighty Chinook or king salmon which averages between 10 and 30 pounds and often reaches over 50 pounds. They are caught from San Francisco to Alaska. The best months are usually from May to September, but in many places they can be caught the year round.

The best way to catch king salmon is by "mooching" with a fresh or frozen herring that is "plug-cut" and impaled on two hooks attached to a leader anywhere from 6 to 8 ft. long. The leader is attached to a keel or crescent-shaped sinker ranging from $\frac{1}{2}$ to 4 oz. It all depends on how deep you must fish and the

A top inshore game fish is the barracuda. They are plentiful in the Florida Keys, the Bahamas and throughout the Caribbean.

Spinning tackle is ideally suited to casting from a small boat in inshore waters.

This 15-pound barracuda, caught off the east side of Bimini, was whipped on a 4½-in. mullet-scale Pal-O-Mine, a 12-in. leader of No. 2 wire, 8-lb. test monofilament line, a Cenature "Pacific" reel and a heavy-duty "Hurricane" rod.

Ray Ovington and Don McCarthy, two expert anglers, admire a bonefish caught in Bahamas waters.

strength of the current or tide. Kings are usually found in water anywhere from 30 to 125 feet or so deep, and you must get down there with your rig and herring bait. The herring must roll slowly like a crippled bait fish as the boat drifts with the tide. When the tide is slack you may have to troll slowly with the motor to give the herring bait the right action.

The best spinning rod for this fishing is one of the special mooching rods about 9 ft. in length made for this work. Mono lines testing from 8 to 20 lbs. are used, depending on the size of the fish running and stiffness of the rod. The rods with flexible tips and stiff butt sections make the best mooching rods.

A somewhat similar variation used for salmon is called "spinning" and here the "spinner" is usually a pennant-shaped strip cut from the side of a herring and hooked with one or two hooks. This should also turn in the current. In this fishing you fish from an anchored boat and cast out your rig behind the boat and hold the strip of herring suspended at various depths, in an effort to locate the feeding salmon. When the tide slackens off or slows you can reel in very slowly and raise your rod tip to give the bait action which attracts the salmon.

Trolling with spoons and plugs will also take king salmon, but here you usually need heavier rods and lines to handle the weights used to get the lures down deep. However, on the occasions when salmon come up to feed near the surface you can often use lighter spinning tackle for trolling.

The smaller but more active silver or cohoe salmon runs from 8 to 15 pounds. Anything over that is a big fish. But no matter what size these silvery streamlined salmon put up a fast fight, often skittering on top or leaping out of the water. They are found from Northern California to Alaska, and feed in bait fish such as herring, needlefish and candlefish around the mouths of rivers and kelp beds. You can often see them chasing the bait fish on the surface. At such times a long, narrow spoon cast among them and reeled fast will often bring strikes. You can use your light salt-water spinning rod for this fishing. They can also be taken by trolling spinning lures, such as spoons and weighted streamer flies, a few feet below the surface.

Another popular family of fishes taken by spin anglers are the weakfishes. The common or northern weakfish is caught from Cape Cod to Florida. Here chumming with live grass shrimp is best and light spinning rods are used to drift the bait, usually a live shrimp or whole sandworm, in the current. You can also catch them in the bays by bottom fishing with strips of squid or pieces of shedder crabs. They'll also hit weighted streamer flies, jigs, spoons, small metal squids and plugs at times.

The southern weakfish, known as the "sea trout," is the favorite from the Carolinas to Florida and the Gulf of Mexico. This weakfish often feeds on top, and popping or torpedo plugs, worked fairly fast to throw a splash, often get them. Sea trout will also strike jigs, underwater plugs and small spoons. Most of them, however, are caught with live shrimp, which can be drifted with the current with or without a cork float or bobber.

Along the Pacific Coast a bigger relative of the Atlantic weakfishes can be caught. He's the white sea bass, which may reach 80 pounds or more. A schooling fish which likes to feed at daybreak and at night, the white bass puts up a good fight on light tackle. However, since these fish are often found around kelp beds, you'll need fairly heavy spinning outfits to keep them from entangling your line in the kelp fronds. The best bait for white sea bass is a live or dead sardine. They will also hit slowly trolled or reeled spoons, metal squids and jigs. Jigging with metal lures is also done down deep, with the lure worked up and down.

When we turn to tropical waters we find a spin fisherman's paradise. In such spots as Florida, the Bahamas, Bermuda, the Caribbean and Mexico, the spin angler will find a large variety of game fish. And most of them can be taken on small lures and light salt-water spinning outfits. The most versatile spinning rod in southern waters is one about 6½ or 7 ft. long which can be cast with one hand. It should handle lures up to about $1\frac{1}{2}$ oz. A small or medium-sized salt-water spinning reel holding about 250yds. of 8-lb. test line is used with this rod. With the lighter rods and smaller reels you can use 6-lb. test.

The glamour fish of tropical waters is the highly publicized bonefish. Noted for their terrific speed and long runs, they are sought by anglers looking for top sport. In United States waters the best place to catch these fish is along the Florida Keys. However, they are more numerous in the Bahamas and parts of the Caribbean, where you can often catch several fish in one day. Hawaii is another spot where they are found.

The bonefish feeds on the flats surrounding the islands in tropical waters. He's mostly a bottom feeder, grubbing in the mud for crabs and other crustaceans. The fisherman locates them by watching for "tails," as the bonefish feed nose down. Or he looks for "muds" or small clouds of muddy water stirred up by the feeding fish. Sometimes they can also be spotted swimming singly, in pairs or small schools. The best way to locate them is by poling a boat on the flats. You can also wade the flats, but less ground is covered in this way. Polaroid sunglasses are a big help in spotting them. If you want bonefish without wasting too much time your best bet is to hire one of the experienced bonefish guides found along the Florida Keys and parts of the Bahamas. If you have plenty of time and patience you can "do it yourself."

The best bait for bonefish is a live shrimp, crab, piece of conch or the meat from the tail of a spiny lobster or crayfish. This can be drifted from an anchored boat when a bonefish is seen moving up. The fish can often be attracted to the boat by chumming with pieces of conch, crayfish or shrimp. You can also pole or drift in a boat and cast the bait in front of a bonefish.

Bonefish will also take a properly presented artificial lure such as a small yellow or white jig, tiny plug or weighted streamer fly. Here you have to cast the lure just ahead of the fish, so that it doesn't frighten him yet is close enough to be seen. In shallow water the lighter lures are best, since they make less of a splash and don't sink as fast. When a bonefish strikes wait a second or two before setting the hook, to give him time to mouth it. When you do hook the fish you'll know it — the line will melt from your reel at an alarming speed. Hold your rod tip high, so that you keep as much line as possible off the water to prevent it from cutting on coral or weeds.

The bonefish is rarely eaten and, unless it's your first fish or an exceptionally big one, the sporting thing to do is to free it so that it can thrill another angler.

Sharing the spotlight in tropical waters with the bonefish is the equally glamorous tarpon. The tarpon under 50 pounds or so is a wonderful fish to hook on light or medium spinning tackle. Over that weight and for fish around the 100-pound class or heavier you'll need heavier rods and lines. But no matter which outfit you use you're not going to land too many fish when using artificial lures. The great majority of the tarpon hooked on lures leap and throw the hook. But it's a lot of fun to hook and fight them, even if you don't land them.

Tarpon, especially the big ones, are usually found in the inlets or passes along both coasts of Florida. As a general rule, the West Coast of Florida has more fish than the East Coast. Along the Florida Keys they are caught in the channels and cuts between the islands and in the deeper holes along the shallower sections. There is often good fishing under and on both sides of the many bridges connecting the different keys. Tarpon also move up the rivers, creeks and canals, where the spin caster stands a chance to land more fish, since they are usually smaller here.

You can hook and sometimes land tarpon on surface plugs, underwater plugs, spoons and jigs. But your best bet to catch one is to fish with natural baits such as crabs, mullet or live catfish. These are fished near the bottom or are drifted with the current. Early morning or dusk and at night are the best times

Spinning tackle makes fishing for such flounders or flatfish a lot of fun.

Who said men have all the fun? Petite Mrs. Pauline Ankney, of San Francisco, Calif., proved otherwise with her 7-ft., 130-pound giant sturgeon, caught on a Mitchell spinning reel and 15-lb. test Platyl monofilament off China Camp in San Francisco Bay. It took Mrs. Ankney nearly two hours to bring the fish to gaff from her skiff. No tall tales will be necessary for fisherwoman Ankney —she got the fish and can prove it.

for tarpon. The spring and summer months provide the best fishing.

A somewhat easier fish to land, but often more difficult to fool, especially a big one, is the snook. They are fairly plentiful in Florida and Mexico. Snook will take surface plugs, underwater plugs, spoons and jigs. As for natural baits, a live shrimp, mullet or pinfish is best. Snook are found in rivers, canals, inlets and along the surf, especially around sand bars, tidal rips, jetties, bridges and piers. They bite best early in the morning, late in the evening and at night.

Another tropical gamester is the barracuda, found in Florida, the Bahamas and the Caribbean. This is the great barracuda, which sometimes reaches a hundred pounds. They strike plugs, spoons, jigs and strip baits. But one of the surest ways of catching them is to use a small live fish on a big hook. Use a wire leader on all the lure or hooks, since they have sharp teeth. You'll find the great barracuda on the reefs, on the flats around islands, in inlets, channels and bays. They are caught all year round but are most plentiful during the summer months.

Then there are the members of the jack family of which the jack crevalle is the best known and most numerous. They'll hit almost anything you throw at them in the way of lures. When you hook one, get set for a long, hard battle—one that will surprise you after you get the fish near the boat or shore and see how small it is. All the members of the jack family fight hard, including the amberjack, permit, blue runner and several other jacks.

The mackerels also put up a good fight and will give your spin outfit a good workout. The common mackerel, Pacific mackerel, Spanfish mackerel and king mackerel are all fine game fish. They will strike such lures as plugs, spoons, metal squids, jigs, flies and such natural baits as live fish, cut fish and strips.

Finally, there are many "bottom fish" which can be caught by the salt-water spin angler. For many kinds of bottom fishing the conventional outfits are more practical, as when fishing around reefs, rocks, wrecks, kelp beds and in very deep water or strong tides. Any time you need a strong line or a lot of lead to get down and hold bottom the conventional reel, stiff rod and heavy line are better. But under many other conditions spinning outfits can be used for bottom fishing.

Spinning outfits have proved their worth for bottom fishing when fishing from bridges, piers, or shore, where long casts are often needed to reach the best fishing spots. Bait fishing with the various natural baits used in salt water is one of the most dependable ways to take bottom fish. With a spinning outfit you can often use 1, 2 or 3-oz. sinkers in shallow waters. For heavier sinkers you'll have to use the heavier spinning rods and lines. Another trick is to add a leader of much stronger line on the end of the main line. Even so, when using sinkers and fishing around reefs, rocks, kelp, sunken wrecks, mussels and other rough bottoms you have to accept the loss of many rigs and fish.

The spinning outfit excels when using artificial lures for bottom fishing. In recent years many spin anglers have discovered that most bottom fish can be caught on bucktail jigs, diamond jigs, spoons and similar metal lures. You simply lower these lures to the bottom and start working them up and down. This jigging attracts most salt-water species, and sooner or later they will grab the lure with their mouths or get hooked in some part of their bodies.

16

Spinning in the Surf

NO GROUP OF SALT-WATER ANGLERS accepted spinning tackle
with more enthusiasm than the surf fishermen — not so much the
old-timers skilled in the use of conventional tackle as the novice
or casual anglers just starting out or those who didn't get a
chance to do much fishing. Before surf spinning rods and reels
appeared it usually meant years of practice before an angler
could become a good caster with a conventional reel. Even the
expert surf anglers with many years behind them often had
trouble with backlashes. So it was only natural that surf anglers
should welcome spinning tackle when it appeared on the scene.
Today you will find surf spinning outfits being used by the great
majority of surf anglers along our Pacific, Atlantic and Gulf
Coasts.

On the Atlantic Coast from Maine to New Jersey the most
popular fish taken in the surf is easily the striped bass. No other
fish has more devoted followers, and striper fishermen will put up
with almost anything to catch a few fish. They fish in storms,
rain, cold, all night just to feel the thrill of a striped bass grabbing
a lure or bait and taking off on a long run. It's a gamble that
sometimes pays off when you run into a school or hook a big
fish. Then you may catch a dozen or more small stripers or land

a lunker weighing 40, 50 or even 60 pounds. In recent years the larger stripers haven't been too plentiful, but there have been great runs of the smaller school fish along the Atlantic beaches. The main appeal in striped- bass fishing in the surf is the challenge—you pit your knowledge and skill against a worthy, crafty opponent.

Striped bass along the Atlantic Coast are caught in the surf from April to November, with the best months usually June, September, October and November. During this period some days are better than others, of course. And on other days the fishing is poor. So surf anglers keep in close touch with the water and fishing conditions. Local tackle stores, surf-fishing friends and the outdoor columns of the newspapers often provide information as to when the stripers are in and hitting.

Stripers usually feed early in the morning around daybreak, late in the evening and at night. They like plenty of surf and white water; so during and after a storm, especially a northeaster along the Atlantic, is a good time to fish for them.

When down at the beach you can sometimes locate the striped bass when you see "breaks" indicating fish are chasing bait fish. Or the gulls and terns may be diving into the water. But most of the time the fish don't show and you'll have to fish blind. Look for stripers around jetties and breakwaters, rocky points, coves and over ledges and reefs. Along sandy beaches they feed on the sand bars, in sloughs and holes. These spots are particularly good if there are strong rips and currents and plenty of white water from breaking waves.

The spin angler should carry a good assortment of lures if he wants to interest Mr. Striper. The old dependable metal squids up to 3 oz. or so are good. The heavy spoon-type lures are also excellent. So are surface and underwater plugs, jigs and rigged eels. Surface plugs are worked fairly fast so that they throw plenty of splash. Metal squids are reeled at different speeds until the right one is found. Underwater plugs are best at moderate speeds.

Of all the fish found in the surf, the striped bass is the most highly prized.

In quiet waters with no surf you can use a light spinning rod. But most surf anglers use medium or heavy rods and big reels because long casts are needed and there is usually some surf or undertow.

Rigged eels and eel skins, which are usually fished at night, are reeled very slowly.

When stripers are running small, from about 2 or 3 pounds up to 15 pounds or so, you can use a medium-weight spinning rod and 10 or 12-lb. test lines. However, when the big stripers come in and heavy lures are used the heavier spinning rods with 15 or 20-lb. test lines are better.

When the striped bass won't take artificial lures they will often go for such natural baits as bloodworms, surf clams, shedder crabs, squid, mullet and live eels. These can be fished with the heavier surf spinning rods and 3 or 4-oz. pyramid sinkers on 18 or 20-in. leaders and 5/0 to 8/0 hooks.

Along the Pacific Coast striped bass fishing in the surf is generally restricted to a few areas. The best-known stretches are the beaches about 100 miles north and south of San Francisco. Some of the beaches are right near the city itself, such as Baker's Beach. The late spring and early summer are usually best here.

The mouths of rivers entering into the Pacific Ocean just north of San Francisco are also good at times, but usually more dependable fishing is found inside the rivers themselves.

West Coast anglers have depended mainly on natural baits, such as chunks of sardine or whote anchovies, in the past. These are used on rigs with hooks running from 5/0 to 8/0, depending on the size of the fish that are around. Pyramid sinkers are best when fishing along the sandy beaches.

In recent years, however, Pacific Coast anglers have discovered that striped bass will often take artificial lures in the surf. This is especially true during the summer months when smelt, on which stripers feed, are present in the surf. Then such lures as metal squids, heavy spoons and plugs will often take them.

Another popular surf fish along the Atlantic Coast is the channel bass, or redfish as he's known in Florida. He is caught from the beaches mostly, from Virginia to northern Florida. Channel bass are also present in the Gulf of Mexico, where they often come in to feed in the surf. Channel-bass fishing is best along the Atlantic Coast in May, June, October and November. In Florida they are often caught the year round, but the late fall and winter months are more dependable. The same spinning tackle used for striped bass is also used for channel bass, although the heavier rods are preferred, since you often have to cast heavy sinkers and big baits. The bait usually used is a chunk or fillet of menhaden or mullet on a 6/0 or 7/0 hook and a pyramid sinker of 3 or 4 oz. The "fish-finder" rig is the most popular, with wire leaders being used if there are bluefish around. Sometimes channel bass will also strike metal squids, spoons, plugs and jigs. Look for them in the surf around inlets, deep holes and sloughs.

East Coast anglers also catch weakfish in the breakers. The common or northern weakfish are taken in waters from Massachusetts to Virgina. The southern weakfish or sea trout is caught below North Carolina to Florida and the Gulf of Mexico. Both kinds of weakfish will take cut mullet, pieces of squid, shedder crab and shrimp, fished with sinkers on the bottom. Use hooks about 3/0 or 4/0 for small fish and 5/0 or 6/0 for larger fish. Weakfish will also take plugs, metal squids, spoons and jigs in the surf.

When a school of bluefish hits into the surf along the Atlantic Coast anglers have a lot of fun and sport. This fishing has been pretty good in recent years but is due to fall off when the blues pull their disappearing act and vanish from our waters for a dozen years or more. In the meantime they can be caught in the surf when they come in to feed. Look for birds working or for bluefish breaking water or chasing bait fish. They will hit metal squids or spoon-type lures best, but surface and underwater plugs and jigs will also take them. Bluefish can also be caught on baits such as mullet, menhaden and butterfish on a wire leader and a 6/0 or 7/0 hook.

There are also many small species which are caught in the surf along the Atlantic Coast, such as the northern and southern

The angler using spinning gear, on the left, is just beaching a nice chinook salmon near the mouth of the Rogue River, Oregon.

Most surf anglers today use spinning tackle when they cast from the beaches. Sunrise and sundown are two peak periods for surf fishing.

whitings, known as kingfish in the north. They bite on seaworms, shrimp, shedder crabs and sand bugs on a small No. 1/0 hook fished on the bottom. Use small baits and your lightest spinning rod for the most fun with these fish.

Another popular surf fish, taken mostly in southern waters, especially in Florida, is the pompano. Sought by thousands of anglers there because of its fine eating qualities, they also put up a fine scrap on light tackle. Use small No. 2 or No. 1 hooks rigged either singly or in pairs on a standard surf bottom-fishing rig. The top bait for pompano are the sand bugs or sand fleas, which are obtained in the wet sand along the surf under the receding waves. Just dig them out with your hands. Run the hook from the bottom up through the top shell. Pompano take these and other baits without nibbling; they swallow them and then take off. They will also hit tiny feather or bucktail jigs at times. The best months for pompano in Florida are from late winter through the spring.

Along the Pacific Coast the croakers, mainly the spotfin and yellowfin croakers, are sought by surf anglers. They are caught from Point Conception, California, south into Mexico. The spotfin reaches a larger size than the yellowfin croaker, usually averaging between one and three pounds. In the surf these fish are found along the sandy beaches and in "croaker holes" or deeper spots. The best season to catch them is during the spring and summer months. Use No. 1 or No. 1/0 hooks for small fish and slightly larger ones for the bigger croakers. The best baits for them are sand crabs, mussels and rock worms.

Another West Coast favorite caught in the surf is the corbina. This fish is similar to the northern and southern whitings found along the Atlantic Coast. But corbina reach a somewhat larger size and longer length. However, they have the same, small, underslung mouth, and require small hooks such as No. 4 or No. 2. The best baits are mussels, rock worms, clams and sand crabs. Look for corbina along sandy beaches most of the time.

They range as far north as San Francisco, but the best fishing is found along Southern California and in Mexico.

Also caught in California, Oregon and Washington in the surf are the surf perches. They are caught in the fall and winter months, as well as most of the year. Although small, they are numerous in species and numbers. They are found mostly around piers, breakwaters, inlets and rocky shores. Since they rarely grow larger than a foot or so in length you can use light spinning rods. Small No. 6 hooks baited with mussels, shrimp, clams, pile worms or sand crabs are used for bait.

Kelp bass and sand bass can also be taken from shore in some places in Southern California, especially where kelp beds are found within casting distance. They will usually take No. 1/0 or No. 1 hooks baited with sardines, anchovies, squid and clams. They are found the year round, but are usually fished from spring to fall.

California anglers also catch some halibut from the surf, but fishing for them is better from piers, bridges and breakwaters where you can reach out into deeper water. They are found in sloughs, bays and lagoons, where they feed on smaller fish. So sardines, herring or anchovies make the best bait, especially if alive. Dead ones will also work if given some action. Cast out and reel in slowly along the bottom.

Pacific Coast surf anglers sometimes get a chance to catch steel-head and salmon, either in the surf at the mouths of rivers or up in the rivers themselves near the ocean. The best runs occur from fall through the winter. On the smaller streams the entrances may be blocked by sand and bars, so steelhead often wait just outside for heavy rains to wash these obstructions away. During this period anglers often take them by casting with spoons, small metal squids and plugs. They are also caught on strip baits and shrimp at times. Here long casts are often required, so the longer, medium or heavy spinning rods are best for this fishing.

This by no means covers all the fish that can be taken by surf spinning. Many other kinds are caught at rare intervals or in certain areas. When you go surf fishing you never really know how small or how big or what kind of fish you may hook. The ocean is full of surprises and that's the basic appeal of surf fishing.

17

Salt-water Offshore Spinning

WHEN SPINNING TACKLE first became popular in salt water it was used mainly for surf and inshore fishing. Few salt-water anglers dared to take the light rods and lines offshore where they might hook the larger and gamier salt-water game fish. Then a few experts looking for new thrills decided to risk their light tackle in the deeper offshore waters. They soon discovered that under the proper conditions they could fight and lick fish of surprising size. Since then such fish as sailfish, marlin and sharks have been conquered on spinning tackle.

However, for every deep-sea "giant" or "monster" there are hundreds of smaller offshore species which can provide fun and sport. Pacific Coast anglers, for example, have the scrappy yellowtail, which average from 10 to 30 pounds and grow up to 100 pounds in weight. Fish going 50 and 60 pounds are taken almost each season. This fishing is most popular in Southern California and Mexico, where yellowtail are most plentiful. Here live-bait boats leave from Ensenada, San Diego, San Pedro, Long Beach, Newport, Balboa and Oceanside. Farther north they may show up around San Clemente and Catalina Islands.

The live-bait boats charge anywhere from $5.00 to $12.00, depending on how far they go and for how long. Some of them

A rabid fisherman who believes that spinning is the only sporting way to take sailfish, Frank Niven of El Monte, California, is shown above with sailfish, dolphin and a torro, all taken at Mazatlan, Mexico. The sailfish tipped the scales at 117½ and 127¾ pounds, respectively. Mullet was used for bait.

One hour and 45 minutes of muscle-weary battle was required before this giant California black sea bass was finally subdued by spin-fisherman Robert Harper of Tustin, California. The big bruiser was taken off the Pacific Coast on 30-lb. test line spooled on a Langley Spinator spinning reel, and officially weighed in at 246 pounds—only one pound short of a world-record catch!

limit the number of anglers. Spin anglers should pick one of the limited boats or those that cater to spin fishermen. The yellowtail season runs from March to November, with April, May, June and July best. Farther south, in Mexican waters, you can often take them the year round.

Yellowtail usually travel in schools and frequent kelp beds. The live-bait boats head for these areas, usually located around offshore islands. Here they chum for the yellowtail by throwing live anchovies into the water. When the fish appear you bait a small No. 4 or No. 6 hook with a live anchovy, sardine or herring. Larger No. 1/0 to No. 5/0 hooks can be used for big "yellows," but generally the smaller the hook the more strikes. The anchovy or other bait fish should be allowed to swim around naturally.

When a yellowtail takes hold and is hooked you have a fight on your hands. The fish almost invariably tries to head for the kelp beds and you either have to stop him or turn him. This, of course, is difficult to do with a light drag used with the lighter spin rods. One bit of strategy is to give the fish slack line in the hope that it will head out into open water. Yellowtail are noted for their long runs, so you will need a good-sized spinning reel with plenty of line capacity. Never try to hold a fresh yellowtail when it wants to run.

The best rod for yellowtail is the special live-bait rod, 9 to 10 ft. long, made for this fishing. The lighter rods of this type can be used with 10 to 15-lb. test lines. The heavier rods will handle lines from 15 to 30 lbs.

Yellowtail can also be taken by trolling or casting near the kelp beds, especially when they are chasing bait fish. The best lures are jigs, metal squids, spoons and plugs.

On many of these same live-bait boats you can often catch albacore and small bluefin tuna. The same tackle and methods can be used as for yellowtail except that when a school of albacore is located you have to work fast and the fish will often take a dead anchovy as quickly as a live one. When the fish "boil" or break behind the boat, get the bait out there fast. Usually the first ones out get fish. An albacore makes fast, long runs, and should be allowed to go freely on a light drag.

Pacific albacore are unpredictable fish, however, and are often hard to locate. They usually appear late in June or July and roam all over the ocean, feeding on schools of bait fish. During the height of the season there are "Albacore Specials," which are live-bait boats with a limited number of anglers that go strictly after albacore. Smaller boats can also troll for these fish with feather or bone jigs. The spinning angler is better off in one of these charter, private or U-Drive boats, since he can fight his fish with less hindrance. Of course, the big problem in the smaller boats is the frequent lack of a big tank where live bait can be kept for chumming when the fish are located.

Another top fish that can be caught from the live-bait boats is the bonito. For them a somewhat lighter rod can be used than for yellowtail or albacore, since they run only up to about 10 or 12 pounds in weight along the Pacific Coast. Lines testing 10 to 15 lbs. can be used with these rods. Bonito will take live anchovies, sardines and mackerel from 5 to 6 in. long. They will also hit feathers, jigs and metal lures, which can be cast from the bow and reeled fast.

These same bonito provide top sport for spinning anglers along the Atlantic Coast. They are often caught there from boats fishing for bluefish off the New York and New Jersey coasts. They are attracted by bunker or menhaden chum and will often take a hook baited with a chunk of bunker or butterfish. Small spearing or silversides and shiners also make good bait for them. At times they will also hit lures such as jigs, metal squids, spoons and plugs in the chum line or when trolled or reeled fast. Bonito along the Atlantic Coast usually go up to 6 or 8 pounds in weight.

While fishing for bluefish or bonito you may attract a school of false albacore. These fish, like the bonito, usually appear in northern waters along the Atlantic Coast during the summer

He's into a yellowtail off the Coronado Islands, reached from San Diego, Calif. More and more spinning rods are being used from the live-bait boats in these waters.

Don McCarthy holds an 8-lb. blackfin tuna caught in Bahamas waters. Offshore spinning for these and bonito, albacore and the mackerels is top sport.

months, with August and September the two best months to catch them. The false albacore will take most of the baits and lures that attract the bonito. For both the bonito and false albacore one of the sportiest outfits to use is a one-handed spinning rod, with a large fresh-water spinning reel or small salt-water model. The line can test about 8 or 10 lbs.

Another popular summer fish along the Atlantic Coast is the bluefin tuna. They appear in July and stay until late September, from Cape Cod to North Carolina. Of course, I'm referring to the smaller bluefins up to about 100 pounds in weight. These are best for spinning tackle. The giant bluefin tuna, weighing several hundred pounds, are for the boys with the conventional gear. School tuna often appear in vast areas, usually from several miles to 40 or 50 miles offshore. They are usually caught by trolling with such lures as cedar jigs, feather lures, metal squids, spoons and strip baits. To interest them you have to move the boat pretty fast, and the lures should be trolled abreast of each other about 20 or 30 feet behind the boat. After you hook your first fish you can often catch more if you keep it in the water until another one is hooked.

If school tuna are running small, say from 10 to 50 pounds, you won't have too much trouble handling them on medium to heavy spinning tackle. But if the fish range from 50 to 150 pounds you'll need the heaviest spinning rods and lines up to 30 lbs. or more to keep the fight from continuing too long and to prevent break-offs. Even then you'll often have to start the motor and follow a hooked fish that is taking too much line.

The smaller relatives of the tuna — the mackerels — often provide good sport for spin fishermen. The Atlantic mackerel, also called the common mackerel, which ranges from Labrador to the Carolinas, is often found in offshore waters. The big ones, especially, stay in the deeper waters. Here they can be attracted to the boat with ground menhaden or bunker and will strike pieces of fish bait or artificial lures such as spoons, metal squids, jigs and flies. They will also take such lures when trolled or cast. Since mackerel reach only a few pounds in weight, the lightest spinning tackle should be used for top sport.

In southern waters another mackerel—the king mackerel—is a great game fish. It can be caught in offshore waters over reefs. It is most numerous around Florida and in the Gulf of Mexico, where anglers fish for them around the oil rigs. In Florida they are caught from charter boats and the open-party drift boats. King mackerel will strike trolled or cast lures, such as feather lures, jigs, spoons, metal squids and strip baits. They will also take natural baits, such as balao and mullet and shrimp. When using any of the lures or baits use a wire leader, since the kings can cut your line with their sharp teeth. King mackerel run up to 100 pounds in weight and fish from 8 to 30 pounds are pretty common. So a medium-weight spinning rod with 12 or 15-lb. test line is about right for them.

Another great game fish found in offshore waters is the colorful dolphin. Their streamlined bodies are an ever-changing pattern of blue, green, purple, yellow and silver. Dolphin range from New England to the Gulf of Mexico along the Atlantic Coast. During the summer months they are often caught off Long Island and New Jersey. However, they are mainly a warm-water fish and are most plentiful around Florida and other tropical waters. In Florida they are taken the year round but are most numerous in the early spring and into the summer months.

Most dolphin are hooked when trolling such baits as feathers, spoons, metal squids, plugs and jigs. They also strike strip baits and whole bait fish, such as mullet, balao and flying fish. They are a fast-moving fish and will hit lures traveling at a good speed. Many are hooked while trolling for sailfish in and along the edges of the Gulf Stream. Dolphin also have the habit of lurking around floating debris, such as boxes, logs, patches of weed, etc. So baits can be trolled or cast around such objects.

The smaller fish, running from 3 to 10 pounds, travel in sizable

This 23½-pound kingfish was caught in Bahamas waters on the light spinning rod shown. They are members of the mackerel family and put up a good fight.

Tom Payne of Los Angeles, exponent of ultralight angling, is shown with a barracuda weighing 8 pounds, 2 ounces, taken with a Langley Spinlite Deluxe spinning reel while Payne was fishing from a California sport-fishing boat off Santa Monica. The fish put up a 30-minute battle with the extremely light tackle before it could be gaffed. The fish set a new record for 1-lb. monofilament line at the time it was caught.

schools, and these can be caught with light spinning tackle. The larger dolphin of from 15 to 50 pounds require heavier spinning tackle. Dolphin also have the habit of following a hooked fish, so if you want continuous action fish two rods and have one fish in the water until a second is hooked. If one fish is kept in the water at all times others can be hooked and a good catch can be made.

Moving up to the larger offshore game fish, we find that quite a few sailfish have been taken on spinning tackle. The Atlantic sailfish is the top sport fish to be taken offshore in Florida waters. There they are caught from many east-coast ports, such as Palm Beach, Fort Pierce, Stuart, Fort Lauderdale, Pompano Beach, Miami and along the Florida Keys. The best fishing is in or along the edges of the Gulf Stream. In recent years more and more sailfish have been taken in the Gulf of Mexico. During the summer months sailfish range as far north as North Carolina, but the best fishing is found during the winter and spring months along the east coast of Florida.

Atlantic sailfish are usually caught by trolling whole mullet or balao or on strips cut from larger fishes, such as bonito. These baits are trolled on top with a skipping motion, to attract the sails. When trolled on outriggers there is a time lapse to permit the sail to grab or swallow the bait. Then the angler can set the hook when the slack is taken up by the moving boat. Lines can be trolled direct from the rod tip, and in such cases the angler must hold the rod at all times, and start feeding line the minute the fish strikes the bait.

When a sailfish is hooked it often takes off on a high leap or a series of leaps. Or it may start tailwalking across the top of the waves. It puts up a game fight to the end and, of course, provides the most sport on spinning tackle. Atlantic sailfish range from 30 to 70 pounds, with an occasional one reaching close to a hundred or a bit more. You can use medium-weight spinning tackle with lines testing from 8 to 15 lbs. if you are a skilled angler. For the beginner, however, a somewhat heavier rod and lines testing from 15 to 30 lbs. are more practical.

The Pacific sailfish is found from Southern California down into Mexican waters. They are more numerous than Atlantic sailfish in many spots along the coasts of Lower California and Mexico and in Panama Bay. Pacific sailfish also grow much bigger, sometimes reaching more than 200 pounds in weight, with fish over 100 pounds fairly common. Pacific sailfish are caught in much the same manner as Atlantic sailfish — that is, by trolling such baits as whole mullet, mackerel, sardines or flying fish on top, behind the boat. The technique of hooking the Pacific sail is also much the same as for the Atlantic species. There should be a 10-second drop back or wait before setting the hook. The spinning angler using light lines must take care in striking, or he'll snap his line in a second. One way to do this is to troll with the drag tension off the reel so that the line can be allowed to peel off when a fish hits. Then, after a 10-second wait, the drag pressure is increased and the rod tip is brought back two or three times, to set the hook.

Although Pacific sailfish over 100 pounds have been caught on lines testing from 8 to 12 lbs., the beginner is better off with somewhat heavier lines, testing 15 or 20 lbs., until he acquires the skill of fighting sails on light tackle.

Somewhat similar to sailfish are the marlins. Along the Atlantic Coast the white marlin is fairly common in offshore waters. They are found along the Atlantic Coast during the summer months from Cape Cod to the Carolinas. Boats sailing out of Ocean City, Maryland, during July and August catch many of these fish. In warmer waters around Florida and the Bahamas they are present from January to July.

In northern waters the favorite baits for white marlin are whole squid and rigged eels. In southern waters they favor mullet, balao and strips cut from the bellies or sides of dolphin, bonito, and mackerels.

In Pacific waters the striped marlin is most plentiful, ranging from California south to Chile. They are very common in the Gulf of California during the spring months. They reach 400 pounds and fish in the 200-pound class are fairly plentiful. The favorite baits for them are flying fish, Sierra mackerel and strips cut from bonito. The baits are trolled in the same manner as for sailfish and other marlins.

The giants of the marlin family are the blue marlin and black marlin. Blue marlin grow up to 1,000 pounds, while black marlin have been caught on rod and reel up to 1,500 pounds, and are believed to grow larger. Of course, at the present time only the smaller-sized marlins are taken on spinning tackle and the biggest ones are reserved for conventional tackle.

Finally, the spin angler venturing offshore shouldn't neglect the sharks. They can provide top sport with the kind of light tackle used by spinning enthusiasts. There are many kinds of sharks and not all of them can be classified as top game fish or sport fish. The species usually recognized as game fish are the mako, the white, the tiger, the porbeagle and the thresher. But other sharks, such as hammerheads and blue sharks, can also furnish some thrills and fun.

Of all of them the top performer is the mako shark. There are two distinct species: the Atlantic mako and the Pacific mako. Both are widely distributed in offshore waters in their respective areas. Makos run fast and leap out of the water, and they are guaranteed to provide enough action for any angler, whether he uses spinning tackle or conventional gear.

Since many sharks reach 1,000 pounds or more, you have to decide how big a shark you want to fight before you select the proper spinning rod, reel and line. Some of the smaller sharks, up to 100 pounds, can be handled on light or medium tackle and lines testing from 8 to 15 lbs. For those going up to 400 or 500 pounds you'll need the heaviest spinning rods, biggest reels and lines testing from 15 to 30 lbs. For sharks weighing over 500 pounds you'd better stick to conventional tackle unless you want to spend hours in a fighting chair.

Sharks require big hooks and long leaders at least 15 ft. long if you want to boat them. Their sharp teeth, rough hides and their habit of rolling and twisting will make short work of a light spinning line. Most sharks bite best at night and come closer to shore at this time. They can be attracted to the boat with chum —a mixture of menhaden or bunker with beef blood creates a slick that will attract sharks from great distances. Almost any small fish or piece of fish can be used for bait. Give the shark plenty of time to swallow the bait before setting the hook.

Many sharks give up quickly and put up a disappointing fight, but some are real scrappers and fight hard and long. When a shark is brought near the boat it must be shot or lanced in the gills so that it can be killed before being brought aboard. Never bring a live, healthy shark into a small boat. Sharks are dangerous until they are stone dead, and even then the shark teeth can give you a nasty cut if you rub bare flesh against them. The safest way to bring a shark in with a small boat is to lash it to the side and tow it in the water.

In most offshore fishing you need at least two men—one to fish and another to handle the boat. You'll find plenty of captains and guides of charter boats in most of our coastal ports who will take you out for this fishing. The cost will run anywhere from $40.00 to $125.00 for the day. This, of course, can be split, if two or three spin anglers chip in to share the cost.

It pays to follow the advice of the captain or his mate about where and when to fish, rigging the bait and hooking the fish. The way the captain or mate handles the boat will have a lot to do with boating a big fish, so close co-operation is a must.

18

Spin-fishing Records

SPINNING OPENED UP a new horizon for both fresh- and salt-water anglers by enabling them to take big fish on the lightest rods and lines. But because spinning was introduced in the United States only after World War II it was several years before anglers could obtain the spinning tackle and gain the experience necessary to go after the different fresh- and salt-water species successfully. Then, in 1951, a group of California fishermen, attracted to spinning and seeing its great sporting possibilities, formed the National Spin Fishing Association. In 1959 this group became the International Spin Fishing Association.

This organization maintains world records achieved with spinning tackle on line classes ranging from 2 to 12-lb. test. It also works on a world-wide basis, through member clubs and individual associate members, to promote conservation of fishery resources by supplying official ISFA rules and regulations for conservation derbies based on releases and on line test versus fish weights.

They have compiled and published a book called the *Tackle Box Record Book,* which lists the world game-fish records on both spinning and conventional tackle. This book, which sells for $1.25, can be ordered from the International Spin Fishing Association, P. O. Box 203, Downey, California. If you want to find out what fish have been taken with spinning tackle on lines testing 2, 4, 6, 8, 10 and 12 lbs. in both fresh and salt water, get this booklet.

When we examine some of the record fish taken on spinning tackle we cannot help but be impressed by some of the big fish taken in both fresh and salt water on such light lines. In fresh water, for example, a 15 lb. 2 oz. large-mouth bass was caught on 8-lb. test line by Emanuel Winters in Lake Tarpon, Florida. Charles D. Jacobs, caught a 12 lb. 12 oz. large-mouth on 6-lb. test line in the same waters in 1960. In the small-mouth bass division Gene M. Schweitering caught a 6 lb. 1 oz. fish in Lac Du Flambeau, Wisconsin, on 4-lb. test line.

When we come to muskellunge one man, Leonard Hartman of Ogdenburgh, N.Y., is in a class by himself. He holds the muskie records in almost all the line-test classes from 2 to 12 lb. His biggest fish were a monster of 59 lb. 13 oz., caught in 1960 on 8-lb. test line, and another of 67lb. 15oz., which he took on 11-lb. test line. He also caught a northern pike of 17 lb. 5oz. on 2-lb. test line. Leonard Hartman does most of his fishing for muskies and pike in the St. Lawrence River in New York.

One of the largest northern pike taken by spinning was the 31-lb. fish taken on 8-lb. test line in Nortdeich, Frankfurt, Germany by Captain R. J. Oostdyke, USAF.

In the trout division, an 8 lb. 8 oz. brook trout was caught on 6-lb. test line by Donnell Cullpepper in Canada. A 14 lb. 7 oz. cutthroat trout was caught by Leonard Hyduke on 8-lb. test line in Walker Lake, Nevada. A 12 lb. 9 oz. brown trout was taken by Dave Uffer in Rio Rimay, Argentina, on 8-lb. test line. A 25 lb. 4 oz. Kamloops trout was caught by Lester H. Lunblad in Lake Pend Orielle, Idaho, on 8-lb. test line. This is the official ISFA record, but back in 1948 Joseph Bates, Jr., famous spinning expert took a 31 lb. 12 oz. Kamloops (a variety of rainbow trout) from Lake Pend Orielle on 8-lb. test line. A 37 lb. 8 oz.

This kelp bass weighing 8 pounds, 3 ounces was caught by Bill Hill on 2-lb. test line.

The "Musky King," Leonard Hartman of Ogdensburgh, N. Y.,
holds a musky caught in the St. Lawrence River. It weighed
67 pounds, 15 ounces, and was taken on an 11-lb. test line and
Mitchell 306 spinning reel. Hartman holds all the muskie records
on the ISFA chart.

lake or mackinaw trout was caught by Richard Newland in Lac La Ronge, Canada, on 8-lb. test line. A 28 lb. 11 oz. steelhead was caught by Rex S. York in the Klamath River, California, on 10-lb. test line.

When we turn to salt water we find some real big fish caught on fantastically light lines—like the 25 lb. 10 oz. albacore caught by William Hill, Jr., out of San Diego, California, on 4-lb. test line. The largest albacore is the 39 lb. 8 oz. fish caught by Dr. R. S. Rubaum off San Clemente Island, California. This fish was taken on 12-lb. test line.

In the amberjack division Karl Osborne caught a 42-lb. fish on 10-lb. test line at Vero Beach, Florida.

A 42 lb. 10 oz. great barracuda was caught by Bill Moeser at Key Largo, Florida, on 12-lb. test line.

In the channel bass division the 60 lb. 8 oz. fish caught by Arthur Clark, Jr., in 1954 at Nags Head, North Carolina, is the biggest recognized by the ISFA. It was caught from the surf on 12-lb. test line. A 62-lb. channel bass was taken on 20-lb. test line by John Twachtman.

The ISFA record for striped bass is a 48-lb. fish caught on 6-lb. test line by John Froehlich in the Susquehanna River, Maryland. Of course, several larger striped bass have been caught on spinning tackle, but they haven't been registered with the ISFA. One of the largest is the 64 lb. 4 oz. striper caught by Louis Katine on November 7, 1958, on 10-lb. test line from the surf at Atlantic Beach, N. Y.

In the bluefish division a 16 lb. 4 oz. fish was caught by Charles H. Johnson at Atlantic Beach, N. Y., on 8-lb. test line.

One of the largest bonefish caught on spinning tackle is the 15-lb. fish caught by Nat Carlin at Islamorada, Florida, on 12-lb. test line.

In the cobia division a 46 lb. 14 oz. fish was caught by Roy Martin at Panama City Beach, Florida, on 10-lb. test line.

In the dolphin division a 35 lb. 3 oz. fish was caught by Robert Bruchez in Mexico. This was on 10-lb. test line.

A 64-lb. black drum was caught by Joseph Bucciarelli at Manahawkin, New Jersey.

A 74 lb. 1 oz. halibut was caught by Paul McDonald in Coos Bay, Oregon, on 10-lb. test line.

A 39 lb. 8 oz. jack crevalle was taken by Bill Lund in Hobe Sound, Florida, on 10-lb. test line. This is quite a feat when you consider the way the jack crevalle fights.

A 32 lb. 8 oz. ling cod was caught by George M. Badalick in Puget Sound, Washington, on 8-lb. test line.

A 43 lb. $\frac{1}{2}$ oz. king mackerel was caught by Eugene Wilhite near St. Petersburg, Florida, on 10-lb. test line.

A 50-lb. roosterfish was taken by Maurice Levy in Mexican waters on 10-lb. test line.

A 56-lb. chinook salmon was caught by Al Weismeyer in Smith River, Oregon, on 12-lb. test line. Buzz Fiorini has taken chinooks in the 53-lb. class in British Columbia, Canada, on 6 and 8-lb. test lines.

In the snook division the 32 lb. 8 oz. fish taken by Roy S. Patten in Boca Raton Lake, Florida, on 8-lb. test line is an outstanding catch.

The 115-lb. tarpon caught by Gus Getner at Port Isabel, Texas, on 10-lb. test line is the biggest on the ISFA chart.

As for yellowtail, the 42-lb. fish caught by Al Zapanta in Mexican waters on 10-lb. test line is one of the biggest taken on a spinning rig.

When we come to the deep-sea giants we find that the 30-lb. bluefin tuna caught by Glenn R. Bracken off Catalina Island, California, is one of the biggest registered with the ISFA. Of course, along the Atlantic Coast school bluefin tuna from 10 to 100 lbs. or more in weight are very common, and there are plenty of records to be broken in this division.

One of the biggest Atlantic sailfish taken on spinning tackle

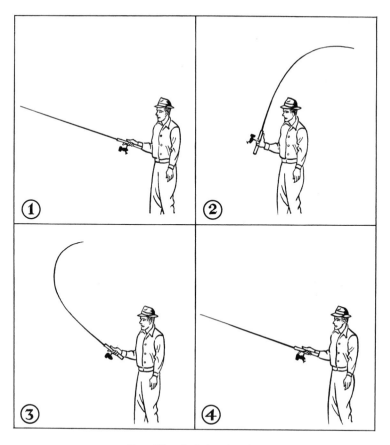

One-Hand Spin Casting

1. *Start cast with rod held slightly above horizontal line, lure close to tip, finger holding line.*
2. *Using wrist, snap rod up to about 1-o'clock position and stop.*
3. *Again using wrist, snap rod forward and down so as to cause bend in rod tip. Finger now releases line for free cast.*
4. *With rod returned to original position, finger stops line against spool lip as lure hits.*

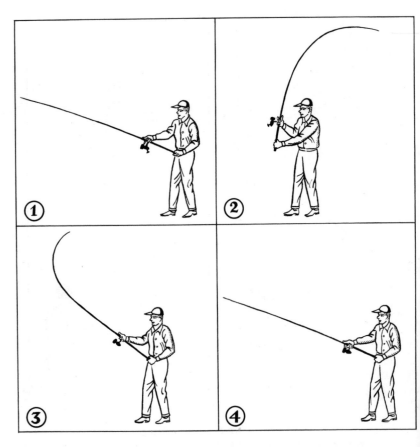

Two-hand Spin Casting

1. *Start two-hand cast with rod in position as illustrated, index finger holding line.*
2. *Snap right arm and wrist upward and back, move left arm forward, and bring rod up to 1-o'clock position.*
3. *Push down sharply with right wrist and arm so that the rod will whip the lure out as finger releases line.*
4. *With rod returned to original position, index finger stops line as bait or lure hits target.*

is the 83-lb. fish caught by Earl Bowers, Jr., at Marathon, Florida, on 12-lb. test line. In the Pacific sailfish division the 145-lb. fish caught by Dr. Earl Hershman at Mazatlan, Mexico, is the biggest in the 12-lb. test-line class.

In the striped marlin division the 183 lb. 7 oz. fish caught by Robert Gaxiola off Guaymas, Mexico, is the top fish. It was caught on 10-lb. test line. The same angler also holds the record Robert Bruchez in Mexico. This was on 10-lb. test line. Guaymas on 12-lb. test line.

In the shark division the mako caught by Charles Meyer, which weighed 261 lb. 11 oz., off Montauk Point, N. Y., is the record. It was taken on 12-lb. test line.

Many larger fish than these have been taken in some of the divisions but have not been registered with the International Spin Fishing Association. You don't have to be affiliated with this organization to enter a world-record fish caught on spinning tackle. You merely pay $1.00 for registration of the record and another 5 cents for the World Record Registration Form to be filled out. But there are many benefits for fishing clubs or individual members who join the ISFA. If you want further details on World Record Registration Forms or membership requirements, benefits and dues, write to the International Spin Fishing Association, P. O. Box 203, Downey, California.